David Lusk

History of the contest for United States senator

Before the 34th General assembly of Illinois, 1885

David Lusk

History of the contest for United States senator
Before the 34th General assembly of Illinois, 1885

ISBN/EAN: 9783337150730

Printed in Europe, USA, Canada, Australia, Japan

Cover: Foto ©ninafisch / pixelio.de

More available books at **www.hansebooks.com**

HISTORY

OF THE

Contest for United States Senator,

BEFORE THE

Thirty-Fourth General Assembly,

OF ILLINOIS, 1885.

By D. W. Lusk,

AUTHOR OF POLITICS AND POLITICIANS OF ILLINOIS.

SPRINGFIELD, ILLINOIS.
1885.

CONTENTS.

CHAPTER I.—BEFORE THE BATTLE, 3—Death of Members, 3—Democrats Confident of Success, 6—Forms of Law, 4—Delay in the Organization of the House, 5.

CHAPTER II.—PRIMARY PREPARATION, 6—Democratic Caucus, 6—Two Candidates, 6—Speech of Mr. Merritt, 6—Speech of Mr. Dill, 8—Speech of Mr. Duncan, 9—Mr. Morrison Nominated, 10—Remarks of Mr. Morrison and Mr. Harrison, 10—Managing Committee, 11—Republican Caucus, 12—Speech of Mr. Whiting, 12—Speech of Mr. Cooley, 13—Nomination of General Logan by Acclamation, 14—His Speech, 14—Managing Committee, 17.

CHAPTER III.—ACTION OF THE RESPECTIVE HOUSES, 17—Joint Assembly, 20—No Separate Ballot for United States Senator in the Senate, 19—Speech of Senator Whiting Nominating General Logan, 17—Senate repairs to the House to meet in Joint Assembly, 20—How this was done, 20—Speech of Mr. Parker Nominating General Logan, 20—Remarks of Mr. Morris, 25—Mr. Linegar Nominates Colonel Morrison, 26—Mr. Johnson, of the Senate, Seconds his Nomination, 27—No Vote, 28—Joint Assembly takes three ballots for Senator, 29—Death of Representative Logan, 30—Death of Senator Bridges, 31.

CHAPTER IV.—AN EXCITING EPISODE, 32—A Bold attempt to resist the Admission of Mr. Weaver, 34—Telegram sent to Washington announcing the election of Lambert Tree as United States Senator, 33—Session of Joint Assembly Protracted until Night-time, 34—Mr. Crafts in the Chair, 34—An Attempt to Corruptly Influence Republican Members, 35—A Persistent Call of the Roll, 35—Mr. Haines takes the Chair, 35—Brave Exposure by Mr. Fuller, 35—A Demand for the Removal of Lobbyists from the hall of the House, 36—Great Excitement, 35—Lambert Tree receives 101 votes and Logan 1, 36—The Speaker declares No Election, 36—Another Recess, 37—Great Excitement, 37—Roll-call, 37—Senator

CHAPTER I.

BEFORE THE BATTLE.

The contest for United States Senator to succeed Gen. John A. Logan, was the most memorable in the history of all the States, extending over a period of full four months. Three times were the deliberations of the General Assembly saddened by death; first a Representative was stricken down in the capitol building, while on his way to attend the morning session; then a Senator was carried away by lingering disease, and lastly, another Representative fell asleep in the night-time, never to waken again in this life. Others, who had been called home by sickness and death, left the dead to bury the dead, and others left the lives of dear ones hanging, as it were, between time and eternity, that they might be present and discharge their duty to their State and the Nation. These interventions of an inscrutible Providence not only confused and prolonged the labors of the Joint Assembly, but spread sadness and gloom over the entire State. Besides these deaths, men, strong men, stricken down by disease, yet anxious to serve the people, were carried from day to day to the hall of the

House of Representatives to take part in the proceedings of the Joint Assembly. The members of the managing committees of the respective parties were kept on the alert day and night watching the whereabouts of absent members, for whom, more than once, special trains were dispatched hundreds of miles.

When the General Assembly first convened, the Republicans had a majority of one in the Senate, and the Democrats one in the House. The Democrats having carried the National election the preceding November, felt confident of their ability to elect a Democrat to succeed Gen. Logan, notwithstanding they lacked one vote to give them the necessary 103.

The Revised Statutes of the United States, providing the time and mode of the election of United States Senators, sections 14 and 15, read as follows:

"The Legislature of each State which is chosen next preceding the expiration of the time for which any Senator was elected to represent such State in Congress, shall, on the second Tuesday after the meeting and organization thereof, proceed to elect a Senator in Congress.

"Such election shall be conducted in the following manner: Each house shall openly, by a viva voce vote of each member present, name one person for Senator in Congress from such State, and the name of the person so voted for, who receives a majority of the whole number of votes cast in each house, shall be entered on the journal of that house, by the clerk or secretary thereof; or if either house fails to give such majority to any person on that day, the fact shall be entered on the journal. At twelve o'clock, meridian, of the day following that on which proceedings are required to take place as aforesaid, the members of the two houses shall convene in Joint Assembly, and the journal of each house shall be read, and if the same person has received a majority of all the votes in each house, he shall be declared duly elected Senator. But if the same person has not received a majority of the votes in each house, or if either house has failed to take proceedings as required by this section, the Joint Assembly shall then proceed to choose, by a viva voce vote of each member present, a person for Senator, and the person who receives a majority of all the votes of the Joint Assembly, a majority of all the members elected to both houses being present and voting, shall be declared duly elected. If no person receives such majority on the first day, the Joint Assembly shall meet at twelve o'clock, meridian, of each succeeding day during the session of the Legislature, and shall take at least one vote, until a Senator is elected."

As there was a division of sentiment in the minds of the dominant party in the House as to who should be Speaker, that branch of the General Assembly was not organized until the 29th of January, therefore the first Joint Assembly could not lawfully meet until the second Tuesday thereafter, but in this case it did not convene until Friday, the 13th of February.

CHAPTER II.

PRIMARY PREPARATION.

DEMOCRATIC CAUCUS.

The Democrats were the first to meet in caucus to put forth their candidate for United States Senator. Many of the leaders felt confident of final victory, notwithstanding there was one vote lacking in Joint Assembly to make victory complete; therefore there was no little struggle and canvass before-hand as to who should be the caucus nominee. In addition to the names of Wm. R. Morrison and Carter H. Harrison, who were foremost in the fight, such eminent men as Wm. J. Allen, John C. Black and Wm. Brown were freely discussed; but when the caucus met Wednesday evening, February 4th, the only names presented were Wm. R. Morrison and Carter H. Harrison. Senator Duncan was made Chairman of the caucus. Senator Merritt nominated Mr. Morrison by saying:

"*Gentlemen of the Caucus:*

"I rise before this Democratic caucus, of 1885, to make a nomination. I have been in about four before this one, but I rise to-night for the purpose of placing in nomination a person whom I expect will receive a majority of the House of Representatives. In placing this person before this caucus I place before you a man who is a native of our State, all of whose interests are in and with the State; a man whose interests have been for the past thirty or forty years identified with those of the State, and marched in line with its progress; a man who, in 1858-9, was Speaker of the House of Representatives of Illinois; a man who used to ride from the Mississippi to Springfield on horseback, carrying the reports of the collector of taxes; a man whom the people have tried and not found wanting; a man whom the Democratic party has found the same to-day, was yesterday, and will be to-morrow, and forever. He also was in the House of Representatives in 1871 and 1872, and under the new constitution, which required new laws and new machinery. He was true and not found wanting. He was in the House when the elements of earth on fire swept Chicago, when thousands were left homeless, and infants born who had not even shelter to cover their heads. He was then a member, and when the Cook County delegation came asking for an appropriation of $3,000,000 to relieve them, and it was lacking one vote, he arose in his seat and voted that Chicago should have it. And then the citizens of Chicago took a portion of the old court house bell and made from it a head for a handsome cane which they presented, accompanied by their grateful thanks, to William R. Morrison. Again, going back to 1846-7, we find him off for the Mexican war, by which we now have the gold-glittering fields of California, the silver of Colorado, and the plains where we pick our rich tropical fruits, and where stock thrives winter and summer. Again, in 1860 he came to the front. He did not wait for Stephen A. Douglas to make a speech, to find out whether or not it was going to be popular to take up the cause, but at the first sound of the drum, he joined an Illinois regiment, which made a glorious record. He is a man who suits all classes of people. He has been a member of Congress and a representative of the party. He is a man who commands the respect and confidence of his party, and I am one Democrat who will vote for him. I will vote for any Democrat who can succeed, no matter who he may be. The time has come when the Democrats can succeed in the election of a United States Senator, and by the eternal gods they shall succeed, and for that reason I now take pleasure in placing in nomination Hon. Wm. R. Morrison."

The speech of Mr. Merritt was warmly applauded, and when silence ensued Mr. Dill said:

"I rise for the purpose of seconding the nomination of Mr. Morrison for United States Senator. Like the gentleman who preceded me, I will vote for any Democrat for United States Senator. I take pride in saying that the Democrats have abundance of material, are in the majority, and will send a representative to Congress. There is the scarred veteran, Black, who would do honor to any people, or Col. Allen, who is fit to represent any constituency, or the talented and learned Judge Snyder, or Carter H. Harrison, who is a thorough Democrat, and has done much for the party; but among the lot there is none more eminently fitted for the position than Wm. R. Morrison. A native of the State; born at a time when log cabins were the order of the day;

a man with a bright and shining intellect which charms the masses; he has, by unquestioned integrity and careful attention to duty, won the respect and confidence not only of the people of Illinois, but of the whole United States of America; a man who, amid all his years of long service in the National Legislature, and the corruption which has so long disgraced the Nation, has come out like the Hebrew children of old, without the smell of corruption. The charge has been made that Mr. Morrison is a free-trader. I would call attention to the fact that Mr. Morrison does not believe in a protective tariff as proposed by the Republicans. He is a tariff reformer, rather. He will treat all people of all classes with equal justice, and I want to say in conclusion that his election will be a credit and honor to the great commonwealth of Illinois, and the people will be proud of him."

Senator Duncan placed Carter H. Harrison in nomination, saying:

"Coming, as I do, from a quarter of the State where I see more substantial political progress accomplished than in any other territory, I assume the high honor of placing in nomination a man whose name has been talismanic with the success of the party. The gentleman whom I will name is one who has done much towards making it possible to send a man to the assistance of the President-elect in the Senate, from this great commonwealth. I claim that this gentleman has done much to make it possible for us to send a Senator to the halls of Congress. He represents the great metropolis of the west, and has made it possible for the Democratic party to succeed where it was a Republican stronghold. The success of the Democratic party in this case is paramount, and we must not throw away this chance of success for the mere pleasure of giving a complimentary vote. I would never strip Mr. Morrison of one laurel which has crowned his success, but it behooves the Democrats not now to put in nomination a man who cannot meet with success. I would not detract anything from Mr. Morrison, but I would ask if it were better for the service of the President-elect to send an actual Senator rather than send him the honor of a nomination. Whoever is the nominee of the convention, I will be with you. I have the honor of placing in nomination before this caucus Carter H. Harrison."

This form over, the balloting proceeded, Mr. Morrison receiving 67 votes, Mr. Harrison 19, Mr. Black 3, and Mr. Schofield 1. Total number of votes cast, 90. There were 12 absentees. Mr. Morrison having received a majority of all the votes cast, Mr. Crafts moved that the nomination be made unanimous, which was done with rousing cheers.

Mr. Morrison being present, acknowledged the honor conferred upon him in these brief words:

"*Mr. Chairman and Gentlemen of the Caucus:*

"Your nomination was neither unsought nor unexpected. Yet were I unmindful and not deeply touched by it, I would hardly be worthy the high trust you have reposed in me. To be the choice of a great political party is always a great distinction. For this evidence of your confidence—this great honor—you have my sincere thanks and grateful acknowledgments. At some more suitable time I will be pleased to say something to you about great public questions. For the present, I thank you all."

Mr. Harrison being also present, responded to repeated calls, substantially as follows:

"*Gentlemen:*

"As I have not the pleasure of thanking you for the honor, I think I may be allowed to rise [standing on a chair] above the floor. I am sure—although he beat me—that I am at least two feet higher than my friend, Morrison. I did want this nomination; but I accept your decree—I'll not say with pleasure, but with great resignation. I acknowledge that the smallness of my vote surprises me. It was unexpected. I didn't think my friend, Morrison, could beat me so badly. Had I been nominated I would have expected every Democrat to have supported me. I felt sure they would do it, and I feel equally sure that all the Democrats will support the man who has beaten me. I ask—not for myself, but for the cause of Democracy—that every Democrat in the two houses will be loyal to the nominee, and vote for Col. Morrison."

There were selected as the Managing Committee, Messrs. James W. Duncan, Thomas E. Merritt, Maurice Kelly, Alson J. Streeter and Elizur Southworth, of the Senate; and Messrs. E. R. E. Kimbrough, C. E. Crafts, Ben F. Caldwell, James M. Dill, Geo. H. Varnell, David T. Linegar, C. C. Johnson and John H. Baker, of the House.

All the forms of organization having been completed, Mr. Morrison went forth in a manly way to win victory, but he was doomed to disappointment, as the sequel will show; for whether the Democrats were to be successful or not, well known Democratic lobbyists had avowed it openly that he should never be the successful candidate.

REPUBLICAN CAUCUS.

The Republican caucus met at the Leland Hotel Thursday evening, February 5th, and on motion of Mr. Fuller, Senator Mason was made Chairman, and there being but one candidate for United States Senator before the caucus, the business of the meeting proceeded at once. Senator Whiting made the first nominating speech. He said:

"*Mr. Chairman and Gentlemen of the Caucus:*

"The task I have to perform is an easy and pleasing one. The nomination has indeed already been made. We are the representatives of the people of the great State of Illinois, sent here to give voice to the wishes of the people. Illinois is rich in great men, as she is rich in products of the soil; but there is one who in civic service and military life stands out; one with high resolve, who will lead us on to victory. That man is John A. Logan. He has been our friend in every ordeal and was ever ready to the call. But he needs no introduction or plaudits from me. I therefore take great pleasure in nominating John A. Logan for United States Senator."

Mr. Cooley seconded the nomination:

"*Mr. Chairman and Gentlemen:*

"I can assure you it gives me great pleasure to rise in my seat and second the nomination of John A. Logan for United States Senator. I feel that when we nominate General Logan we name a man who will stand by the principles of the Republican party in the future as he has for the past twenty-four years. I believe when we nominate him we but voice the wishes of nine-tenths of the Republicans of this State. I doubt if there are half a dozen Republicans in this State who, if they had an opportunity, would not vote to send John A. Logan back to the Senate for the next six years. He has been found true at all times, and not found wanting under any circumstances—always brave in fighting for the Republican principles as he was fighting in the war. It was always "come, boys," with him, and never at any time did he say "go." We have seen him leading on the Republican party as one of its heads in the presidential contest. In that fight he did more for his party than any other one man in the State of Illinois. It is our duty to give him this nomination, and the people will say we have done well. Gentlemen of this assembly, there are 102 of us in this Legislature, and if we stay together as we should, John A. Logan will be the next United States Senator from this State. We can do so. This is going to be one of the most remarkable fights ever made in this State, and it may be weeks before it is settled. Logan can lead us on to victory, and for that reason I am for Black Jack Logan, and take pleasure in seconding his nomination for Senator."

In the light of to-day, it may be said that Messrs. Whiting and Cooley spoke with prophetic words.

Senators Thompson, Morris and Clough spoke with earnestness in support of the nomination of Gen. Logan, and Messrs. Hamilton, Pike, Fowler, Scharlau and Headen, of the House, spoke briefly in a like vein, when, on motion of Mr. Fuller, the nomination of John A. Logan was made by acclamation and by a rising vote.

On invitation, General Logan addressed the caucus as follows:

"*Mr. Chairman and Gentlemen of the Caucus:*

"I have been notified by the committee that I have been unanimously nominated as your candidate for the office of United States Senator. For this mark of confidence reposed in me by the Republicans of this Legislature and their constituents, I return to you my most grateful thanks, and I shall ever feel gratitude in my heart for this kindness and generous recognition. I desire to say to you that for the many kindnesses I have received at the hands of the people of Illinois, I shall ever be grateful. I owe them a debt of gratitude that I can never have the power to repay.

"Whether I have discharged the duties imposed upon me by the people of this State in such a manner as to be gratifying to my constituents, is for them, not for me, to say. Whether I have at any and all times risen to the standard that has been fixed for me in the line which I have traveled, by their sanction, is for them, not for me, to decide. Of this much I feel conscious, that in all the duties that I have had to perform in official stations, no matter where, in the field or forum, I have discharged them to the best of my ability, and as faithfully and honestly as I could do. And for this renewal of confidence and esteem, again I return my grateful thanks.

"There is but one word I desire to say in reference to this contest. The Legislature, politically, stands equally divided. Sometimes people feel it incumbent upon them to say we cannot elect. Would it not be as well for us to say we will not let the other side elect? I mean by votes; I do not mean by any revolutionary means. Would it not be well for us always, in a contest, instead of thinking that we may be defeated ourselves, to remember at least that the other side may be defeated? Whether we achieve victory now, or not, depends upon ourselves.

"I have known in battles that have been fought, where the troops, our officers would say, are tired; our army is shattered; our lines are broken; our battalions are demoralized. It is not when you are speaking of yourselves that you want to talk that way, but look to the enemy and see if they are shattered and broken, and if their camp is not surprised as well as our own. It is always best to look on the bright side. If we have 102 and they have 102, how can they beat us, if we stand together? This is a contest that may be short or it may be long. The probabilities are, it may be long. If it is, then it becomes a question of pluck and endurance. I never commanded in the field where I had equal numbers that the enemy got the advantage of me. This, now, is a question that perhaps philosophers can solve, but it strikes me this way: The Republican party was defeated in the last National contest. It was a very close one. We yielded without a murmur. We now, in Illinois, are approaching the second contest between Republicans and Democrats. This, now, is a question whether or not the Republicans can stand defeat. If the Republican party stands in a solid, united column, it cannot be defeated now or at any future time; but, if it is going to break up into threes and fours, and in dozens, each one for himself, the Republican party will go to fragments, and will not achieve victory. I do not mean this as a plea for personal success; I mean my remarks to apply to the party. If it stands together in Illinois and elsewhere, and leaves its quarrels behind, the Democratic party has gained its last victory for many years to come. If we do not succeed we may blame ourselves.

"Now, gentlemen, returning to you my thanks again, I have said about all I desire to say. I have no more interest in this contest than you have—not one solitary atom. Of course I would like to be elected, and, if you stand by me, I will be, and I will not be elected by any dishonorable act on my part, or by permitting it on the part of any of my friends. I will in this contest win, in my judgment, the approbation of men of honor by an honorable course. I want no office if it has to come to me by dishonorable means, or if it comes to me by bargain and intrigue; and so help me God, if I should have to agree to condone criminal offences for an office, I would ask heaven to strike me with a thunderbolt. Gentlemen, I thank you again for your kindness and your generosity, and I hope that in this contest, for the benefit of the Republican party, you will lead us to success."

Messrs. H. A. Ainsworth, Geo. E. White, W. C. Snyder and Daniel Hogan, of the Senate, and Charles E. Fuller, Henry C. Goodnow, Abner Taylor, J. B. Messick and W. F. Calhoun, of the House, were made the Managing Committee, and it may be said they cheerfully accepted General Logan as their chosen leader, and determined to follow him to victory, if victory could be won by honorable means.

CHAPTER III.

ACTION OF THE RESPECTIVE HOUSES.

When the House met on the morning of the 10th of February, acting in conformity with the law of the United States, a ballot was taken for United States Senator, but the Senate did not observe this form of law on that day; but on the 13th of February, Mr. Whiting moved that the Senate proceed to the election of a United States Senator, and, pending the motion, nominated Gen. John A. Logan, speaking as follows:

"*Mr. President and Gentlemen of the Senate:*

"In obedience to the constitution and laws of the United States, we now lay aside our legislative work and commence upon the work of choosing a Senator to represent the State of Illinois in the National Congress. The dignity and transcendent importance of the occasion press every heart. We are about to confer upon one of our citizens distinguished honor and grave responsibilities. The brief history of Illinois is adorned with great names, and the living present is no disparagement to the proud record. Each of the several parties in Illinois has worthy representatives, who would honor their State in this high position. Our starry firmament is thickly studded with great names of merit and renown, but there is one which shines resplendent for his civic and military services, his long experience in public affairs, and, above and crowning all, for his high character for integrity, fidelity to the people, and devotion to the public interests. Some of that heroic bravery he brought to every battlefield is often needed in civil affairs, and when so needed, Logan is at the front. The reëlection of Logan can be no mistake. He has been tried in every ordeal, and proved equal in every emergency. The recent election and canvass proved his wide popularity throughout the country, and we all know that at home, if the popular voice could be made potent, he would be borne to the high office on a tidal wave of popular enthusiasm. The people of Illinois are deeply imbued with the spirit which animated Lincoln, and which so gloriously triumphed over slavery and rebellion. They will tolerate no reactionary movement. Accident and political blunders have weakened our power as represented in the General Assembly, and the scale is trembling in the balance. But the throbbing of the hearts of the people is felt through the many avenues of intelligence, and the beat is healthy, steady, and strong for Logan. In the name of my political associates in the Senate, in the name of the men and women of Illinois who have proved their devotion to freedom, equal rights and true progress, and in the name of the patriotic soldiers who watch the contest with deepest interest, I merely give voice in naming John A. Logan as their candidate for Senator. Senators, I ask your attention a moment longer. This is the fourth time I have participated in a Senatorial election with General Logan as the Republican candidate—beginning in yonder former capitol. This is the third time in this capitol the high privilege and great honor have been accorded me in the announcement of his candidacy. During this long period I have been an attentive observer of public affairs. The name of Logan grows brighter with time and service, and on this august occasion I feel the deepest conviction that the true interest and glory of our State and Nation demand the return of Logan to the Senate. If this General Assembly shall do little else but elect Logan, our return to our constituents will be greeted with plaudits, and the accents of that fervent and burning patriotism which animates the hearts of the people of Illinois. The fame of Logan is assured. The most brilliant and thrilling pages of our history are illuminated with his deeds and labors, yet his native State demands his longer services. His ripe experience, united with the most vigorous manhood, promises that to his glorious past shall be added an illustrious future. Republicans of the General Assembly, by honorable means and the blessing of heaven, Logan shall be his own successor."

No other nominations or speeches were made, and no vote was had, because of the breaking of a quorum by the Democrats, and at 12 M. the

Senate proceeded to the hall of the House of Representatives to take part in the first meeting of the Joint Assembly.

JOINT ASSEMBLY.

The Joint Assembly met for the first time on the 13th of February. As the Senate approached in a body, the Speaker announced "the Honorable, the Senate." First came the Sergeant-at-Arms, then the President and Secretary, who were followed by all the Senators except Messrs. Ruger and Streeter. When the roll-call of the two houses had been completed, the Senate, by its Secretary, and the House, by its Clerk, the presentation of candidates to be voted for for United States Senator being in order, Mr. Hilon A. Parker, on behalf of the House, in an easy and graceful manner, placed in nomination Gen. John A. Logan, in the words following:

"*Mr. Speaker, Gentlemen of the General Assembly:*

"In placing a gentleman in nomination for the high and responsible position of a representative in the Senate of the United States, of the proud State of Illinois, I deem it most fortunate that I am able to present one without whose name the history of our State could not be written,—one without whose name the most sacred traditions of that history could not be rehearsed,—a name so interwoven with the principal events of that history, so linked with all that is glorious, heroic and valuable in that history, that to mention the one is to record the other, and to forget the one is to dim the lustre of all.

"It is unnecessary to repeat to any gathering of the sons of Illinois the story of the life and services of Gen. John A. Logan. But, sir, without attempting to do this in detail, it may not be amiss to briefly allude to the salient events in that life, not because they are unfamiliar to any, but because the lessons they teach cannot be too often repeated, and because the pride of State, the devotion to principle, and loyalty to country which they inspire, cannot be too often invoked. Born upon the soil of Illinois at a time when those advantages which are now the pride of our State were unknown, he was deprived of many of those privileges which are often such potent factors in determining leadership among young men in rural communities. Yet, the quality of leadership was so marked in his character, and was so early developed, that we find him at the age of twenty elected as one of the officers of that little band which marched away from their native country, in 1846, to take part in the war with Mexico. He served through that war with credit to himself, and with an ability which secured him advancement in rank and his assignment to high positions of trust. Returning home in 1848, he took up the study of the law, and in 1851, was admitted to the bar, he, meanwhile, having been honored by an election to the position of clerk of his county. In the year following his admission to the bar, he was selected to fill the very responsible position of prosecuting attorney for the then third judicial district of the State.

"In 1852, he was elected to the House of Representatives, and served in that branch of our General Assembly, continuously, until 1856, having served also in the latter year as presidential elector.

"In 1858, he was elected a member of Congress; was reëlected in 1860, resigning his seat in 1861 to serve his country in a wider and more dangerous field of duty.

"In 1866, he was again elected to Congress as a member-at-large, receiving the unprecedented majority of nearly 56,000 votes. He was reëlected to the Forty-first Congress, and in 1871, was chosen to the position of United States Senator, and served in that capacity his full term, which ended in 1877. In 1879, he was again elected to the United States Senate, and his term of service will expire on the 3d of March next.

"This, sir, is a hastily drawn outline-sketch of the civil record of Gen. Logan; and in all of these various positions to which he has been called during the last forty years by the people, he has always been a tireless worker, a true patriot, a safe, practical statesman. There never has been a time in all of these years when he was not implicitly trusted by his colleagues, his constituents, and by the entire country; and to-day he stands in the vigor of life, worthy the post which he has served so well—the one man whom, of all others, the people would trust for the future. He stands the chosen candidate of that party which, for a quarter of a century, has not only guarded well, but which has carried forward, the sacred ark of human liberty and human hopes—the chosen candidate of this party to be his own successor in the highest councils of the Nation; and so universally does the opinion prevail, and so deeply grounded is the belief that the people of the State desire his return to the Senate, that were it possible, and were it proposed to delegate back to the people the right of choosing their Senator by a popular vote, not a friend of Gen. Logan would oppose, and not an enemy but would object. And now, sir, with his ability unquestioned, his experience almost unparalleled, and his integrity above the breath of suspicion, I feel at liberty to speak of other services of this distinguished man, which will ever endear him to all who love their country, and who prize its honor. Nay! I make no excuses, I offer no apologies, for speaking of him in connection with those times, the mention of which will send the memories of many upon this floor trooping backward across the stretches of twenty years, to the days when we gave the elbow-touch of duty in the wild scenes of death and danger; memories which will start the deepest emotions, tugging at the heart-strings of all who have learned the deep, true meaning of the word 'Comrade.' In 1861, when the demon spirit of human slavery was first revealed to the American people, and men stood aghast at the terrible revelation, some there were who quailed and cowered before the coming test of the Nation's strength. Not so with Gen. Logan. Like the spark to the powder-train was the first gun at Sumter to his impetuous nature. He left his seat in Congress to take part in the first considerable battle of the war, bearing the musket of a private soldier. Then resigning his position as a member of ·Congress, he returned to his native State, enlisted a regiment of volunteers, and at its head he entered the field, and from that field he never returned until every armed foe had been driven from it, emerging at the close of the war wearing the bright stars of a Major-General, and the proudest record won by any volunteer officer.

"Turn back the pages of your country's history to where are recorded the noblest deeds performed during the second heroic epoch of our

Republic, and there you will find his name written in letters of unfading brightness. To remember Belmont, Donelson, Pittsburg Landing, Port Gibson, Champion Hills, Vicksburg, Resaca, Kenesaw, Atlanta, and the grand sweep from the mountains to the sea, from the Tennessee to the Potomac, is but to remember the troops of the invincible Fifteenth Army Corps and their ever victorious commander, with their legend of 'Forty Rounds and Always Ready.'

"Say you these are tales which have been told, and they mean nothing to us now? Gentlemen, I would rather be remembered as the lowest private, who marched in the rear rank of the poorest of those regiments which, under the leadership of the aroused Logan, fell upon Hood's lines like an avenging fury that day at Atlanta, when the spirit of the noble McPherson went to its reward, than to hold the place reserved in history for those who, however prominent, however blessed with wealth, and power and station, would bring here, either for themselves or others, their petty spites, their selfish hopes, their real or fancied wrongs, as excuses for failing to perform their present duty to themselves, their State and their country.

"The enemies of our land come no more in battle array; we no longer judge of a man's loyalty to the Nation by the color of his uniform, but these times, as all times, have their dangers and duties, and brave men are always wanted; and if ever fearless men were needed upon the floors of Congress, the occasion is near at hand.

"Return Gen. Logan to the United States Senate, and from all over this broad land there will roll up such a shout of gladness from men whose voices once mingled in swelling the battle's chorus, that those tattered emblems of our martial glory, stored in yonder Memorial Hall, will tremble in their places as if touched by the phantom hands of those who once waved them aloft in the smoke of carnage, and died for their honor.

"Sirs, could the spirit of him whose shadowy form now looks down upon us from these walls— the sainted martyr, Lincoln, whose fame and honor have burst the confines of a State, overleaped the barriers of a Nation, and now girdle the round world with a halo of glory—could he but speak to us this day, who can doubt but he would say what my unworthy lips now repeat: Republicans of Illinois, stand firm! Acquit yourselves worthily! Fight bravely and to the end! Hold not until you have honored yourselves, honored your State, honored the past, and have well prepared for the future, by again placing in his old position of trust, that trained statesman, that courageous leader, that knightly soldier, the tried, brave and true John A. Logan."

The remarks of Mr. Parker were received with ringing applause, and when it had subsided, Mr. Morris, on the part of the Senate, seconded the nomination of General Logan in language that was both forcible and eloquent, characterizing him as the leader of the glorious cause of Republicanism, that by his manly bearing he had won immortal renown and lasting honor. He reviewed his military achievements in vivid language, and said he was the soldier's friend and the idol of the colored race. In all his relations of life, General Logan had never been found "horizontal," but always and forever "perpendicular." In the name of the veteran soldiers, in the name of the commonwealth, he seconded the nomination of the bravest, best, grandest and most courageous statesman of the day.

Following Mr. Morris, Mr. Linegar nominated Col. Wm. R. Morrison. He said:

"I do not desire to pluck one laurel from the brow of Gen. Logan, nor say one word in disparagement of his honor, character, and nobility as a man, soldier and statesman; but Morrison, too, took a stand at the front in the Mexican war, and Morrison, too, has been found where the shell and shot were thickest, where the carnage was greatest, when the terrible war cloud of secession and disunion swept from the Atlantic to the Pacific, and from the great lakes to the gulf. Morrison is a veteran in the political service of his country, and stands to-day in his bold, proud position of a true, upright statesman, who has served his country for more than a quarter of a century, and can say what no other living statesman in America can say—that after a quarter of a century of public service he has not one single vote or act recorded that he would desire to change to-day, if he had the opportunity."

After a warm criticism of Mr. Morris for his reference to the "horizontal" bill, Mr. Linegar concluded his remarks thus:

"When you see the candidate whom it is my honor to present to this assembly, whom do you see? I will tell you. You see simply a citizen of the great State of Illinois, and when you see that citizen you see, so far as his acts and conduct are concerned, one of the proudest statesmen that America has ever produced. I have the pleasure of presenting the name of William R. Morrison."

Mr. Johnson, of the Senate, seconded the nomination of Col. Morrison in an eloquent and happy extemporaneous speech. In the course of his remarks he referred to Gen. Logan as a man of unquestioned military ability and honor.

Of Mr. Morrison, he said:

"I do not desire to pluck a single bud from Logan's laurel wreath, but there was another man who, when his country called in 1846, donned the vestment of a private soldier of his country and native land, and marched beneath the flag across the plains of Mexico, and ceased only when the American flag perched in victory above the domes and halls of the Montezumas,— and that man was William R. Morrison. And again, when the dark clouds of war arose from every horizon, and the National Constitution was in danger and our American institutions tottering, Col. Morrison did not hesitate a moment as to what his duty was, nor consult party technicalities, but, listening to the voice of him whose picture rests there [pointing to the portrait of Douglas], the great leader of the Democracy of the northwest, he donned the uniform of the soldier and marched to the battle-fields of the south, remembering the cardinal principle of Democracy, that the Union is one and inseparable. The country found him true then, true during the war, and thank God he is true to-day. While we can recount the military glories and military services of these great men, while it is right and proper that the past should not be forgotten, it is only right and proper that we should draw lessons from that past to teach us our duties now and in the future. We live in the present and look and labor for the future.

* * * * *

"Gentlemen, with a confident belief that the voice of the Joint Assembly will, in the end, approve our choice, we present the name of William R. Morrison—not less true in Congress than when he marched beneath the flag on the field of Donelson."

This closed the nominating speeches, when the roll-call of the two houses followed, the Speaker directing that as the name of each member was called he should rise to his feet and declare the name of his choice for the Senatorship; but no one voted, notwithstanding the first roll-call showed 200 members present--50 Senators and 150 Representatives. The Speaker, holding in his hand a slip of paper showing that no votes had been cast, promptly announced: "The rolls have been called and no person has been voted for for Senator. No one has been elected, and there is no election." And the first meeting of the Joint Assembly then adjourned until 12 o'clock February 14th.

The Joint Assembly continued to meet from day to day until the 18th without anything like a full membership being present, on which occasions there was but one vote cast for Senator, and that was by Mr. Haines for Wm. R. Morrison. But on the 18th the roll-call showed the presence of 202 members, and this was the first time either party seemed willing or ready to vote as a whole. John A. Logan received 101 votes, Wm. R. Morrison 94, Elijah M. Haines 4, scattering 3. This vote ended the struggle for that day, the Republicans retiring with happy faces, while the friends of Mr. Morrison seemed thus early to realize what had been offensively asserted by certain persons interested in the success of some other candidate in the Democratic caucus, "that Mr. Morrison had secured the caucus nomination, but that he could never be elected United States Senator." On the 19th every member of the respective houses was present, and three ballots were taken that day. On the first John A. Logan received 100 votes, Wm. R. Morrison 94, E. M. Haines 4, A. E. Stevenson 1, Andrew Shuman 1, Elihu B. Washburne 1, scattering 3. Total 204. The second and last ballots were the same. On the 20th all the members were again present, when three ballots were taken. On the first John A. Logan received 100 votes, Wm. R. Morrison 95, E. M. Haines 2, Andrew Shuman 1, A. E. Stevenson 1, Elihu B. Washburne 1, scattering 4. Total 204. On the second ballot John A. Logan received 100, Wm. R. Morrison 97, E. M. Haines 2, Andrew Shuman 1, Elihu B. Washburne 1, scattering 3. Total 204. On the third and last ballot John A. Logan received 101 votes, Wm. R. Morrison 98, E. M. Haines 2, Elihu B. Washburne 1, scattering 3. Total 204. From the 21st of

February to the 25th, inclusive, there were no test votes cast, the party having the most members in attendance on the respective days only voting. On the 21st and 24th Logan received 100 and 101 votes, respectively, and on the 25th two ballots were taken, Morrison receiving 98 votes each time, E. M. Haines 1, John M. Palmer 1, and scattering, 2 each ballot.

On February 26th it was expected that every Republican would be in his seat when the Joint Assembly met, and from certain indications from dissatisfied members on the Democratic side it was confidently believed that Gen. Logan would be elected; but while the Managing Committee was busily engaged in marshaling the Republican forces for the conflict, the word came on the wings of the morning that Representative R. E. Logan was dead, when the hope of success vanished like a meteor. Mr. Logan had been suffering for years from occasional attacks of heart-disease, and died in the line of his duty, just as he had reached the Capitol to take part in the proceedings of the Joint Assembly. From this time to the 11th of March there were no tests of party strength, the Joint Assembly meeting from day to day, and only one side voting. On the 12th the roll-call showed 202 members present. Six ballots were taken on this occasion. John A. Logan received on the first 99 votes, Wm. R. Morrison 99, John C. Black 1, E. B. Washburne 1, E. Nelson Blake 1, scattering 1. Total 202.

On the second ballot Logan received 99, Morrison 98, Black 1, Washburne 1, Blake 1, scattering 1. Total 201. On the third Logan received 100, Morrison 98, Black 1, Washburne 1, scattering 1. Total 201. On the fourth Logan received 100, Morrison 98, Black 1, Washburne 1, scattering 1. Total 201. On the fifth Logan received 100, Morrison 99, Black 1, Washburne 1, scattering 1. Total 202. On the sixth Logan received 99, Morrison 99, Black 1, Washburne 1, Blake 1, scattering 1. Total 202. When the result of this ballot was announced the Joint Assembly adjourned. This was the severest and most protracted test that had yet been exhibited between the opposing forces. Gen. Logan polled within two votes of his full party strength, while Morrison came within three of the full strength of his party. Thus far the contest had been alike honorable on both sides, and there seemed to be no telling how it would terminate, yet the leaders of both sides appeared to feel equally sure of victory in the end. But from the 13th of March to the 20th the Joint Assembly met only formally. No interest was taken in the proceedings by the Republicans. On the 20th of March, Senator Bridges, who had gone home, died, and then followed a long and tedious routine labor of the Joint Assembly until May 14.

CHAPTER IV.

AN EXCITING EPISODE.

On the 14th of May, the Democrats rallied every man on their side of the house with the hope of winning victory out of defeat. Representative Shaw, a Democrat, had died April 12th, and the Republicans had succeeded in electing a Republican in his stead in a district which had given, at the election the preceding November, a large Democratic majority. In the other special elections no change had taken place in the political complexion of the members chosen, but the election of a Republican from this stronghold of Democracy, gave the Republicans a majority of one in the House, and thus secured for them a majority on joint ballot whenever the new member should be seated. This unexpected change in the political situation rendered the leaders of the Democracy absolutely desperate, and hence a determined effort had been planned by them to end the contest in their favor before the new member should be seated. The entire vote of the Democrats was now but 101, but it was baldly asserted that when the proper time came no less than three Republicans would desert

the standard of Gen. Logan and cast their votes for the election of the Democratic candidate, whoever he might be. It was arranged that Col. Morrison, when the Joint Assembly met, was to receive the full vote of his party, and then his name was to be withdrawn, and that of Judge Lambert Tree substituted, when it was confidently expected that Tree would be elected before the close of the day's balloting. So certain were some of Mr. Tree's friends that he would be elected, that a telegram was sent that evening to Washington, D. C., announcing his election, and it appeared in some of the eastern dailies next morning. Accordingly, when the Joint Assembly met on the 14th day of May, the roll-call showed 200 members present, every Democrat being in his seat. On the first ballot Wm. R. Morrison received 99 votes, John C. Black 1, T. E. Merritt 1. Total 101. Mr. Streeter voted for Black, and Mr. Haines for Merritt. The Republicans refrained from voting. On the second and third ballots Wm. R. Morrison received 101 votes. On the fourth Wm. R. Morrison received 51 votes, Lambert Tree 2, John C. Black 2, A. E. Stevenson 1, John M. Palmer 1, Carter H. Harrison 14, R. W. Townshend 5, Wm. J. Allen 7, Wm. M. Springer 1, Wm. Brown 10, scattering, 6. Total 100. During this ballot Mr. Duncan, of the Senate, withdrew the name of Mr. Morrison. On the fifth ballot Morrison received 7 votes, Tree 35, Black 3, Palmer 3, Harrison 10,
—3

Townshend 2, Allen 5, Brown 10, Lyman Trumbull 1, scattering, 22. Total 98. On the sixth, Morrison received 1, Tree 89, Palmer 1, Harrison 1, Allen 1, scattering, 3. Total 96. When the result of this ballot was announced, the Joint Assembly took a recess until 7:30 P. M.

The object in protracting the session of the Joint Assembly was to prevent the seating of Mr. Weaver, the successor of Mr. Shaw, who had arrived late that afternoon, and stood ready to take the oath of office; but the Democrats had determined to resist all attempts to seat him. Thus far the Republicans had been only earnest, patient watchers of events. Gen. Logan, with his brave and trusty marshals, was everywhere plainly to be seen by all in that vast assemblage, which filled the galleries and every available space on the floor of the House.

Such was the condition of matters when the Joint Assembly met at 8:30 P. M., Mr. Crafts presiding. On the first ballot Mr. Morrison received 5 votes, Tree 91, Townshend 1, scattering 3. Total 100. Mr. Haines not voting. The Republicans refrained from voting. On the second ballot, after all the Democrats had voted, Mr. Crafts continued to have the House roll called for absentees, evidently with a hidden purpose. When the roll-call was proceeding for the fourth time, Mr. Fuller vigorously protested against it as being unprecedented, and asked Mr. Crafts how many times he proposed to call the absentees. Mr. Crafts insolently replied, "As long as any one desires to vote," when he directed that the call proceed, but before it was concluded, Mr. Haines, who had been occupying the Speaker's room, came in and took the chair amidst great applause on the Republican side. When order was restored, Mr. Fuller arose and said, amid sensation and great excitement:

"*Mr. Speaker:* There is a rule in the House, and I suppose it applies to the Joint Assembly as well, that only members are allowed on the floor. While I was over on the other side of the house a while ago, I saw a man who is not entitled to the privilege of the floor, but who was lobbying among the members. He is a lobbyist, and I overheard him making a proposition, and trying to unduly influence the vote of a member of this House."

Here followed cries of "Who is he!" "Name him!" "Put him out!"

The excitement was intense on the Republican side, and members jumped from their seats as quick as thought to the side of Mr. Fuller, who pointed to ex-Treasurer John Dunphy, of Chicago, who was standing at the extreme right, as the man whom he meant as having attempted to corrupt members. Dunphy, with a face as red as a comet, stood for a moment staring at the man who had been bold enough to charge him with committing an act which warranted his expulsion from the floor of the House, but not an officer stirred to enforce the rule.

Mr. Merritt tried to ridicule the idea that undue means were being attempted to be used, but indignant Republicans would not hear him. Mr. Whiting said:

"It is as plain as the sun in the heavens that there is an effort being made to buy a seat in the United States Senate."

Mr. Fuller said if there was no other way of removing from the hall persons not entitled to its privileges, he would move an adjournment of the Joint Assembly, but the Democrats would not listen to an adjournment.

The Speaker then announced the result of the second ballot: "Tree 101, Logan 1. Total 102. No quorum voting and there is no election of United States Senator."

This announcement was received amid almost painful silence, the Democrats hoping that Tree would be declared elected, and the Republicans fearing such a result.

The third and last roll-call began quietly, and progressed throughout without any undue excitement. No one voted but the Democrats. When the roll-call had been concluded, it was suggested by Mr. Ainsworth that it be verified, which being done without objection, the Speaker announced the result: "Tree 100, Morrison 1. Total 101." Mr. McNally voted for Morrison.

Here followed a vigorous effort by the Republicans to secure an adjournment, but the Democrats forced a recess until 8:30 A. M., May 15th. This ended the most critical crisis of the long contest. The corruptionists who had thronged the floor of the House made haste to depart, evidently feeling that they had been but poorly rewarded after the confident boast that they had purchased the votes of three Republican members, who would desert the standard of their gallant leader that night; but to the fair name of Illinois, the Republicans stood firm, and resisted the great temptation, which was to leave an imperishable stain upon the reputation of the Thirty-fourth General Assembly of Illinois.

When the Joint Assembly convened at 8:30 A. M., May 15th, the roll-call showed 198 members present. The Democrats had arranged for continuing the session until Sunday, if necessary, in order to prevent the admission of Mr. Weaver to a seat in the House. If they could not elect Tree, then he was to withdraw. But the Republicans were not to be outgeneraled in broad daylight, and they determined to end the session of the Joint Assembly, and compel the seating of Mr. Weaver. Before the proceedings were opened Mr. Weaver's credentials were presented to the Speaker, who remarked that he would "accept service." The roll-call was then proceeded with. When the name of Mr. Ruger, who was not in the hall, was reached, Mr. Merritt answered for him. Republican Senators interposed an emphatic protest, when the President of the Senate directed that the roll be called again, which being done, the answer was not repeated. When the last name on the House roll-call had been called, Mr. Fuller obtained the floor, and said: "Mr. Speaker, I desire to have the name of Mr. Weaver called. He is a member of the House of Representatives, duly elected. He has taken the oath of office, and has presented his credentials to the Speaker of this body. He wants to be recorded."

The Speaker—"Everything in order, according to the Apostle."

Mr. Fuller—"I insist that the calling of Mr. Weaver's name is in order."

The Speaker—"The chair takes notice. No rights will be lost. Let us see where we are, before we take in any strangers."

Here Mr. Weaver took a place at the side of Mr. Fuller. The Speaker insisted upon announcing the result of the roll-call, but Mr. Weaver proceeded, amidst great excitement, to say:

"*Mr. Speaker:* I come here as a duly elected member of the House of Representatives. I have the Governor's certificate, and have taken the oath of office in this chamber. I have presented my credentials to the Speaker, and I ask that he direct the Clerk of the House to call my name."

During the delivery of Mr. Weaver's remarks the Democrats were very noisy, but when he had concluded, Mr. Mason got the floor and forced attention. The prolongation of the Joint Assembly last night, by taking a recess, he said, was no more nor less than an attempt to disfranchise the voters of the Thirty-fourth district. He demanded that no business be transacted till Mr. Weaver answered the roll-call. The alleged recess in the afternoon was for the sole purpose of giving a chance to influence men by corrupt means to desert their party. When the sun was in the sky they could not do it, but had to wait for the cover of darkness. Now they would try to prolong the joint session again till night, when they would again renew their nefarious work. He ended his speech by moving that Mr. Weaver be recognized. The Speaker said he had examined the credentials, and they were correct, but the admission of Mr. Weaver must be in some formal way. Mr. Linegar interposed a motion that the Joint Assembly proceed to ballot, and tried to have the previous question ordered. The Republicans demanded that the journal of yesterday's proceedings be read, making the point that the legislative day could not be extended, as the Democrats had sought to do. The Speaker ruled that there was no yesterday's journal of the Joint Assembly, as that body was still in session. The Republicans appealed from the decision, and on the roll-call refrained from voting.

The hour of 10 o'clock having arrived, which being the regular hour for the meeting of the House under the rules, Mr. Fuller raised the point that the Joint Assembly could not be in session. He cited the case of Senator Harlan in the Thirty-fourth Congress. Harlan went to the United States Senate with proper credentials from the Speaker of the House of Representatives and the Governor of the State of Iowa. The State Senate had adjourned from Saturday till Monday. The Joint Assembly met Saturday, and it was on this vote that Harlan was declared elected. His seat was contested, and it was shown that the State Senate had adjourned from Saturday till Monday, but that in an alleged Joint Assembly Harlan had received a majority of the votes. The United States Senate ousted him on the ground that there could have been no Joint Assembly in session, and consequently no election.

The Speaker thought that this was probably before the present law of Congress was enacted; that whatever was done by the Illinois Legislature would probably be reviewed by the United States Senate, but he thought the only thing in order was a ballot for Senator.

Mr. Mason called attention to the fact that the Senate adjourned last night to meet at 10 o'clock to-day. That hour having arrived, he thought the President of that body should call it together in its own chamber.

Here ensued a tremendous uproar on the Democratic side, but the President of the Senate finally gaining the attention of the Joint Assembly, said:

"On retiring from the Joint Assembly last night, the Senate adjourned till 10 o'clock this morning. It is now the duty of the Senate to proceed to the Senate Chamber and resume its business."

The Republicans greeted this announcement with great applause, while the Democrats became very much excited, demanding that the Clerk of the House call the Senate roll. The Republican Senators then left the hall in a body, being followed by two or three Democratic Senators. When order was restored, Mr. Fuller demanded that the Speaker call the House to order, and that the regular business be proceeded with. Great confusion again ensued. The Speaker recognized Mr. Keyes, who argued the legality of the recess of the Joint Assembly. Mr. Linegar was next recognized, and he talked against time till near the hour of noon.

Mr. Fuller again called the attention of the House to the fact that Mr. Weaver was there, and just before noon tried to get in a motion that his name be placed on the roll, and that the Clerk be directed to call it. The Speaker refused to put the motion, declaring that Mr. Linegar had the floor. "Then," said Mr. Fuller, standing on his desk, and in a loud voice, "if the Speaker refuses to put that motion, I will do it. Those in favor, say aye."

There was a loud response of ayes from the Republican side, but when he put the negative side of the question there was no response from the Democratic side, and Mr. Fuller declared the motion carried unanimously. Here the Democrats became bewildered. They did not know what to expect next. There was great excitement all over the house, but more especially among the Republicans. Just then the tall form of Mr. Messick was seen advancing down the aisle on the Republican side, and when within a few feet of the Speaker, shaking his fist at the Speaker, he declared in a tone that was distinctly heard all over the hall: "Not another vote will be taken for Senator until Mr. Weaver is recognized and accorded his rights. Mark that."

The sentiment expressed by Mr. Messick was fully echoed by all the Republican members, and no vote was taken until Mr. Weaver was seated. The Senate having returned, and while the roll-call was being proceeded with, some of the more conservative Democrats seeing that the Republicans were determined to meet revolution with revolution, advised the abandonment of the attempt to keep Mr. Weaver longer out of his seat, and after some consultation between the Managing Committees of the respective parties, when the roll-call had been finished, Mr. Duncan, speaking for the Democrats, stated that an agreement had been made by which there was to be a practical suspension of balloting until next Tuesday, which was assented to by Mr. White, on the part of the Republicans. The roll of the Joint Assembly was then called, but no one voted, and the Joint Assembly adjourned. The Speaker then called the House to order, when Mr. Crafts called up the credentials of Mr. Weaver, and moved that he be duly installed as a member of the House.

Mr. Weaver had, at the suggestion of some of Gen. Logan's legal friends, taken the oath of office in the hall of the House of Representatives, as prescribed by the constitution, the evening before, which was administered by Judge Wm. L. Gross. With this knowledge, Mr. Fuller said he had no objection to having Mr. Weaver re-sworn. The oath was again administered by Judge Gross, and Mr. Weaver took his seat amid cheers by both Republicans and Democrats. The ugly feeling had evidently died out, and the House quietly adjourned.

Gen. Logan had been constantly on the ground, and in close consultation with Republican members during the long and protracted Joint Assembly, and had advised his friends to keep their heads clear and their hands clean.

A great crisis had been passed. The attempt to secure the election of a United States Senator through corrupt means had been happily averted, and honest men rejoiced.

The Joint Assembly only formally met on Saturday and Monday, the 16th and 18th of May, but each side was all the while busily engaged in getting ready for Tuesday, which all believed would end the contest one way or the other.

CHAPTER V.

LOGAN'S ELECTION.

When the Joint Assembly met at high noon, May 19th, every member was in his seat, ready for the last grand struggle which was to end the long and heated contest for the Senatorship. Gen. Logan was present, his eyes glistening with unusual brilliancy, watching every movement with the same intensity that characterized him in leading a bloody charge on the battle-field. Col. Morrison sat unconcerned in the midst of the Democrats, while Judge Tree was seen moving carelessly about the outskirts on the Democratic side. The galleries were filled to the utmost with ladies and gentlemen, and all the available space on the floor of the House was literally packed with anxious spectators.

When the roll-call had been concluded, the Speaker remarked that it might be important to know what the rules of the Joint Assembly were understood to be, and, in order that there might be no mistake, he would state them. On the vote for Senator, he said, there would be but one roll-call of absentees, but a member not having voted on either the regular call or the call for absentees, would have the right to vote at any time prior to announcing the result of the ballot. The right to change one's vote would be observed in the same way. The President of the Senate then directed the Secretary of that body to proceed with the roll-call of Senators. Mr. Adams being the first on the list, responded distinctly, "John A. Logan." So did Mr. Ainsworth. When Mr. Bell's name was reached, there was no response, which was taken by the Democrats as the cue not to vote. The roll-call proceeded without interruption, every Republican Senator voting for John A. Logan. There was wild applause on the Republican side. The Speaker suggested that there was a necessity for keeping order; that these demonstrations were out of order and might do harm. After specially requesting the bystanders to remain quiet, the Speaker directed the Clerk to proceed with the roll-call of the House. As in the case of the Senate roll-call, the Democrats refrained from voting, but one by one the Republicans voted for John A. Logan until the name of Mr. MacMillan was reached, but the Clerk did not give him time to respond before proceeding to call another name. But Mr. MacMillan was on his feet in an instant, and recorded himself distinctly for John A. Logan. Here was a suppressed cheer on the Republican side, which Gen. Logan silenced by a mere shake of the head and wave of the hand. The incident called out a pleasant remark from Mr. Merritt, and the suspense of the occasion under which all seemed to labor was somewhat relieved by the Speaker's replying that everything was going well and no rights were being lost. When the name of Mr. Sittig was reached, he did not vote. There was a death-like quiet as the roll-call proceeded to the end. When the absentees were called, the Democrats still refusing to vote, every eye in the House was turned toward Mr. Sittig, who, when his name was reached, asked the privilege of explaining his vote; but all uncertainty vanished when he had concluded a speech of fifteen minutes with the words, "I vote for John A. Logan." This gave Gen. Logan the necessary 103 votes, when the wildest shouts of applause rent the hall from the Republican side. Here was a picture for the pencil of a Nast. Handkerchiefs waved, hats went up, and Gen. Logan was tossed about as though he had been a child, while the hand of Sittig was shaken again and again by delighted Republicans. The Democrats had looked on in amazement, and were anxious for quiet. After making himself heard, the Speaker remarked, with some seriousness, that the proceedings of the Joint Assembly were not yet concluded, and that some mistakes might happen which would require correction.

The Democrats now demanded to be recorded, but, under the rules laid down by the Speaker at the outset, the absentees could not again be called, and now the Democratic members of the House proceeded to vote in irregular order, just as they could claim the attention of the Speaker or Clerk, all voting, with only an occasional exception, for Lambert Tree. Mr. Taylor, of Adams, declined to vote at all. Then there was a little parley among the leaders, and Mr. Baker, from Moultrie, mounted his desk, and, getting the Speaker's attention, said:

"I wish to change my vote from Lambert Tree to Charles B. Farwell."

This was taken as a signal for a general stampede from Tree to Farwell, the rallying cry being, "Anything to beat Logan." But this role was soon checked by the Democratic member from Calhoun, Mr. Barry, who, rising in his seat and speaking at the top of his voice, said, "I change from Lambert Tree to John A. Logan." The Republicans greeted this with loud applause, and Mr. Barry was pulled about by the Democrats in every direction, and while under the severest pressure he changed his vote from Logan to Tree. In making the change, he said:

"I want to be in harmony with my party, but I want to see everything done fairly here. I give notice that before any Republican shall take this election away from John A. Logan I will vote for Logan."

All the Democrats of the House changed from Tree to Farwell except Messrs. Barry, Dill, Linegar and Prickett. When the absentees of the House had finished voting, Mr. Linegar rose and asked the clerk how he was recorded as voting, and when told that he was recorded for Lambert Tree, he said:

"I wish my vote to stand as it is."

Mr. Linegar was unwilling that Gen. Logan should be defeated either by a trick or bribery.

The absentees of the Senate then commenced voting, and when nearly all had voted for Mr. Farwell, Mr. Barry again rose in his seat and said, "I change to Gen. Logan." After the applause which followed this announcement had subsided, the Speaker explained that the time for changing would be when the verification of the roll-call commenced. Four of the Democratic Senators declined to change from Tree to Farwell, Messrs. Gore, Merritt, Rinehart and McNary.

Mr. Farwell had received 21 votes in the Senate and 72 in the House. Total, 93.

Finding that the followers of Gen. Logan, not excepting a single personal friend of Mr. Farwell, were immovable, the Democrats then desiring to correct their record, again changed their votes from Farwell, as follows: Tree, 96 votes,

SENATORIAL CONTEST. 49

Black 2, Morrison 1, Hoxie 1, Scholfield 1. Total, 101. This was announced by the Speaker to be the last opportunity for changing.

When the final roll-call had been adjusted on what was the 118th ballot of the last session of the Joint Assembly, the roster stood thus:

Those in the Senate voting for John A. Logan were Messrs. Adams, Ainsworth, Berggren, Campbell, Clough, Cochran, Crawford, Curtiss, Evans, Funk, Hogan, Leman, Mason, Morris, Ray, Rogers, Ruger, Sellar, Snyder, Sumner, Thompson, Torrance, Tubbs, Wheeler, White, Whiting —26.

Those in the House voting for John A. Logan were Messrs. Allen of Johnson, Allen of Vermilion, Baird, Barger, Bassett, Bogardus, Boudinot, Boutell, Boyden, Breckenridge, Brown of Edwards, Brown of Ogle, Buchanan, Calhoun, Campbell of Kankakee, Castle, Chapman, Clay, Cleaveland, Collins, Cooley, Fowler, Fuller, Gittings, Goodnow, Goodspeed, Graham of Henderson, Greenleaf, Hamilton, Hanna, Harper, Headen, Hiatt, Hood, Humphrey, Hunter, Ingalls, Kennedy, Kerr, Kinsey, Lawrence, Logsdon, Long, MacMillan, McCord, Messick, Miller, Morgan of Washington, Nowers, Oldenburg, Orendorff, Parker, Francis W., Parker, Hilon A., Pike, Pollock, Powell, Prunty, Rogers of Jackson, Rodgers of Warren, Ruby, Scharlau, Sheffield, Sittig, Snyder, Spafford, Stassen, Stewart,

—4

Struckman, Sundelius, Taylor of Cook, Thomas, Tontz, Trexler, Unland, Weaver, Whittemore, Yost—77.

Those in the Senate voting for Lambert Tree were Messrs. Bell, Cantwell, Cloonan, Darnell, Davis, Duncan, Forman, Galbreath, Gillham, Gore, Hamilton, Hereley, Higgins, Hill, Johnson, Kelly, McNary, Merritt, Orendorff, Organ, Rinehart, Seiter, Shumway, Southworth—24.

Those in the House voting for Lambert Tree were Messrs. Baker, Barry, Bez, Bickelhaupt, Brachtendorf, Browning, Caldwell, Campbell of Hamilton, Cherry, Choisser, Cleary, Considine, Crafts, Cronkrite, Davis, Dieckmann, Dill, Dorman, Downs, Graham of Macon, Heim, Henry, Hoffman, Hummel, James, Johnson, Keyes, Kimbrough, Langford, Linegar, Mahoney, Marshall, Massey, McAliney, McClung, McDonald, McEvers, McGee, McHale, McLean, McNally, Mileham, Moore of Brown, Morgan of Will, Morris, Mulheran, Murphy, O'Donnell, Paddelford, Patrick, Pearce, Prickett, Quinn, Raley, Schlesinger, Sharp of Bond, Sharp of Wabash, Sheplor, Shup, Stevens, Sullivan, Taylor of Adams, Templeman, Varnell, Watercott, Webber, Weir, Welch, West, Wiley, Winslow, Haines—72.

In the Senate John C. Black received the vote of Mr. Streeter, and in the House that of Mr. Gray—2.

In the House John Scholfield received the vote of Mr. Highsmith—1.

In the House Wm. R. Morrison received the vote of Mr. Moore, of Clinton—1.

In the House John R. Hoxie received the vote of Mr. O'Shea—1.

The Speaker then, with a wearied air, said: "Gentlemen, are you through?" There being no response, he proceeded to announce the result of the vote as follows: "Logan 103, Tree 96, Black 2, Morrison 1, Hoxie 1, Scholfield 1. Total, 204." Pausing a moment: "Of which number John A. Logan has received a majority. Therefore I declare him duly elected United States Senator."

Again the outburst of applause was uncontrollable, Democrats as well as Republicans rejoicing. When order was restored, Mr. Fuller moved that the Speaker appoint a committee of three to conduct the Senator-elect to the Speaker's stand, which being carried, on the second of Mr. Hereley, Messrs. Merritt, Fuller and Chapman were appointed as such committee, and as Mr. Merritt and Gen. Logan proceeded arm in arm to the presence of the Speaker, everybody seemed to shout at the top of his voice. The greeting between Gen. Logan and the Speaker was extremely pleasant, and when introduced to the Joint Assembly, Gen. Logan spoke as follows, amid frequent cheers:

"*Gentlemen of the Joint Assembly:*

"I congratulate you on having brought to a conclusion this most remarkable contest which has been going on for nearly four months. I have no words in which to express my gratitude to the Representatives of this great State of Illinois for the compliment they have paid me to-day. Having been elected for the third time to represent this great State in the Senate of the United States, I hope I have so acted and deported myself in the position before as to bring no discredit upon myself, my party, State and country, and my past history is the only guarantee I can give for my future course. From the deepest recess of my bosom I again thank you for the honor you have conferred upon me. There is no position on earth which could be more gratifying than to represent this great State. In this contest, Mr. Speaker and gentlemen, which has been an unusually close and heated one, I am proud to state that nothing has transpired to mar the friendly relations existing beween myself and my worthy opponent. For thirty years this gentleman and myself have been friends, and I trust we shall always continue such. I believe there never has been a contest between two persons waged more earnestly for their parties than this, and the mutual relations remain so pleasant. I respect Mr. Morrison politically and socially, and I am proud to say we are friends, and sincerely hope we may ever be friends. As to the other gentleman who was my opponent for a time, I can say nothing against him, nor would I want to. Mr. Tree and myself lived neighbors for many years in Chicago, and I have always had the highest respect for him. He made as good a contest, coming late into the field, being a little short of votes, as he could make. For him I have nothing but respect.

SENATORIAL CONTEST. 53

"In conclusion, gentlemen, I desire to say that, no matter what may have occurred during this contest, it has been carried on in a spirit of fairness. No such contest has ever been known in this country before, and it has appeared strange to me that there has been so little excitement and bitterness exhibited. It is remarkable, I say, in a contest which has lasted so long and been so close, that there is so little bitterness of feeling displayed; and I desire to say that, in representing the people of the State of Illinois in the United States Senate, I shall ever try to do that which seems to me to be my duty, representing my party and my constituents fairly and honestly. I leave here having no bitter feeling towards any one who may have opposed me. I respect a man who will stand by his creed and his friends, and I expect no more from others than is accorded to me. If I go to Washington, I do not go there with any fire burning in my bosom or a feeling of antagonism toward any party or the present administration. I shall endeavor to represent you fairly and honestly, and stand by you, all of which I believe is right. Gentlemen, again I thank you. I tender you my most profound thanks. I have not before, nor can I, repay you for the manner you have stood by me in this Legislature and State. I shall ever remember it, and endeavor to prove worthy of the trust you have this day confided to me. Thanking you again, I hope you will learn in the future that the wrong man has not been elected."

At the conclusion of Gen. Logan's remarks, the Speaker addressed briefly the Joint Assembly, saying that he had tried to preside in a way to suit both sides, and expressed the belief that

everybody's rights had been respected. He
thanked every one for the consideration shown
to him as a presiding officer. Then, on motion
of Mr. Hogan, the Joint Assembly adjourned
sine die.

Recurring to the nature of the contest for
Senator, there has never been one of the same
duration or magnitude since the organization of
the National Government. When it became
known that the Thirty-fourth General Assembly
was a tie, then it was that the political corruptionists of Chicago, led by Joseph C. Mackin, attempted, by the most brazen fraud ever instituted, to
cheat the Republicans out of a State Senator,
and thus change the political complexion from a
tie to a Democratic majority. But when Governor Hamilton refused to issue the certificate of
election to the person whom they had counted in
by fraud, then these same men set themselves
about to corrupt Republican members, and when
the General Assembly met, it was boldly avowed
that Gen. Logan could never be elected; that he
had neither money nor the promise of offices to
influence votes. They were bold to say that
while Col. Morrison might never listen to the use
of dishonorable methods to secure his election,
when his name was withdrawn, as it would
be, then they would buy enough Republican
members to secure the election of a Democratic
Senator. The sequel shows that they meant all

and even more than they were willing to say in public. But to the honor of the men composing the Republican majority, be it said, they nobly resisted the tempter. Great offices from the administration at Washington, and more than $50,000, were to be the considerations of Republican betrayal; but by remaining true to principle, true to themselves, and true to their State and Nation, the Republicans set an example that will live as a shining mark for ages to come. We do not write this through prejudice or passion, but because it is the truth of history. Honest men everywhere, Democrats as well as Republicans, may well rejoice that the diabolical plot was not consummated.

No Spartan band ever followed a gallant leader with more courage and loyalty than did the Republican members of the Thirty-fourth General Assembly adhere to the fortunes of Gen. Logan.

CHAPTER VI.

AFTER THE BATTLE.

No election for Senator has ever taken place in the United States where the result gave such universal satisfaction; nor has there been one which attracted so wide-spread attention.

Gen. Logan's able and manly canvass in the Presidential contest of 1884, had won for him a great number of new admirers all over the United States. No sooner had the news of his election flashed over the wires than congratulatory telegrams and letters poured in upon him and his wife from every quarter, South as well as North. Democrats as well as Republicans rejoiced that the "wrong man had not been elected." His rooms at the Leland Hotel were the scenes of the wildest joy, and this was kept up until a late hour at night. Thousands of people gathered in the streets around the hotel that night with banners and music, and would not leave until Gen. Logan had addressed them in the open air.

Gen. Logan remained at Springfield until noon Saturday, May 23d, when he was conveyed in a special car over the C. & A. railway to Chicago, where he was tendered a reception and banquet at the Grand Pacific Hotel.

Douglas, in his palmiest days, never had a more triumphant march than had Gen. Logan on his way to Chicago, nor a more glorious reception than he received that night in honor of his great victory.

The next step in the way of rejoicing over Gen. Logan's success was a grand reception and banquet, given by the Union League Club of Chicago on the evening of May 26th, the following account of which is taken from the *Tribune:*

UNION LEAGUE CLUB BANQUET.

There was a large assemblage at this banquet. One hundred and fifty covers were laid in the main dining-room of the club in the Honoré Building. The room was gaily festooned with flowers and richly draped with the National colors. The tables were arranged along the sides of the room in the form of a square, with four smaller tables in the center.

J. McGregor Adams, the President of the club, presided at the dinner, with the distinguished guest of the evening on his right. Seated at the main table, besides the Senator and the President, were Senator Sabin, W. N. Evans, Joseph Medill, E. G. Keith, J. A. Connolly, J. L. Thompson, Gen. Schofield, Roswell G. Horr, George E. Adams, Dr. Stryker, Dr. A. E. Kittredge, A. L. Coe, M. H. Wilson, John B. Hawley and E. B. Sherman.

The others present were:

R. S. Tuthill, Gen. H. H. Thomas, J. S. Belder, John Jones, R. Silvey, Eugene Cary, Judge Sidney Smith, Edwin Walker, A. Williams, H. H. Belding, J. L. Woodward, G. B. Shaw, Thomas Kane, H. M. Sherwood, T. D. Cunningham, Isaac E. Adams, N. H. Blatchford, C. F. Gates, O. W. Clapp, H. S. Towle, C. K. Offield, M. A. Farwell, D. H. Hammer, J. L. High, W. H. Harper, O. D. Wetherell, L. L. Bond, F. Beidler, Charles W. Tobey, F. B. Tobey, S. D. Kimbark, D. Kelly, G. R. Blodgett, G. W. Matthews, J. S. Rumsey, E. J. Marsh, T. H. Brown, Jr., George C. Miln, P. T. Pettibone, Sr., T. W. Brophy, J. L. Beveridge, J. H. Nolan, J. H. Raymond, W. W. Boyington, T. C. MacMillan, D. V. Purrington, Geo. C. Prussing, Hermann Raster, E. R. Brainerd, W. C. Grant, J. Nevins Hyde, W. L. B. Jenny,

O. Lockett, J. B. Sniffen, O. F. Bane, H. A. Rust, C. F. Gunther, L. McWilliams, V. Falkenau, George M. Clark, J. C. Stirling, J. H. Lang, J. K. Edsall, H. J. MacFarland, W. J. Chalmers, D. W. Irwin, C. T. Trego, W. F. Studebaker, P. E. Studebaker, G. N. Culver, L. L. Coburn, S. E. Barrett, L. Schlesinger, S. M. Moore, G. F. Bissell, G. L. Close, P. P. Heywood, James McKindley, Martin Beem, J. M. Oliver, J. B. Bradwell, W. B. Mitchell, L. F. Burrell, T. C. Clarke, H. H. Walker, H. Watson, Jr., W. V. Jacobs, R. L. North, A. C. Bartlett, W. E. Mason, A. M. Jones, F. W. Palmer, Leonard Swett, A. M. Pence, J. Rosenthal, R. W. Dunham, J. F. Finerty, D. F. Cameron, A. B. Taft, J. J. Parkhurst, L. Manasse, R. S. Critchell, A. J. Harding, T. Van Voorhis, J. O. Wilson, Granger Smith, C. E. Mantz, M. Seiz, A. L. Dinger, L. B. Bane, H. C. Clement, G. W. Hoffman, A. McCoy, R. E. Jenkins, H. M. Bacon, J. B. Leake, C. R. Corbin, J. B. Jeffery, J. W. Parter, D. F. Crilly, G. K. Dauchy, W. H. Turner, F. M. Blair, E. Foote, Jr., J. E. Wilson, E. C. Wilson, W. E. Frost, Lyman Baird, Albert Hayden, S. J. Glover, A. G. Garfield, H. M. Singer, I. G. Lombard, E. F. Craigin, G. F. Harding, L. W. Yaggi, J. J. West, M. Nelson, A. B. Meeker, A. Taylor, U. Balcom, J. A. Roche, Judge Anthony, W. B. Howard, C. R. Cummings, L. W. McConnell, R. A. Keyes, A. Officer, W. Northup, J. H. Hamline, H. C. Eddy, E. Olson, M. Pamlis, L. H Sweet, W. S. Scribner, J. A. Sexton, J. W. Palmer, W. M. Luff, F. B. Bond, J. F. Morse, F. E. Morse, Milward Adams, N. H. Swartout, A. B. Raymond, Charles Catlin, M. V. Burchard.

Dr. Kittredge said grace briefly, after which an hour and a half was spent in the discussion of the menu.

ADDRESS OF MR. ADAMS.

At 11 o'clock President Adams called the banqueters to order, and said:

"*Gentlemen:*

"We have met this evening to do honor to a distinguished citizen. The Hon. John A. Logan has been returned to the Senate after a contest of four long months—a struggle that promises to become historic. While party feeling has run high, we have to congratulate our State that the fight has been conducted in an honest, manly fashion. We welcome our guest to-night, proud that he belongs to our State, our city, and the Union League Club of Chicago. We honor his sterling integrity and his fearlessness in attacking a wrong. Looking at him as a soldier—the hero of Atlanta—or standing in the Senate Chamber battling for days against a flagrant wrong, or at Springfield wisely consulting his friends who have stood by him so long, we admire the qualities that do honor to the soldier, the statesman, the counselor. We tender to him our best wishes, and express the congratulations we feel that he has been returned to his field of usefulness, to serve us in the future with the same steadfastness of purpose as in the past. Gentlemen, I have the honor to present to you Senator John A. Logan."

SENATOR LOGAN'S SPEECH.

After the subsidence of the applause which greeted Senator Logan when he arose, he spoke as follows:

"*Mr. Chairman and Gentlemen:*

"I would be less than a man if I should fail to appreciate the compliment extended to me on this occasion by the Union League Club of Chicago. This club is an association of gentlemen, whose primary purpose is to aid in the preservation of the integrity of the Union and to promote the prosperity of all the people by an honest administration of the Government. These objects should have the endorsement of every honest citizen, and I hope I may be believed when I declare they are most dear to my own heart. I feel the strongest attachment for my country. My most fervent prayer is for its prosperity and permanence. I have from my earliest manhood exerted my best energies and abilities in its behalf. If in so doing I have failed in any degree in securing the approbation of my fellow-citizens, I have at least the consolation of knowing that the rectitude of my intentions has not thus far been called in question. It is not my purpose to enter into the history or details of our recent Senatorial contest. Neither shall I speak of the trials through which we passed or the perils which were averted. Suffice it to say that the victory is ours. To the steadfastness of our people and the integrity of the Republican Representatives in our Legislature is the credit for our success due. I wish to disclaim the idea that the gatherings of people at the different towns and villages along the road from Springfield to Chicago, and the grand reception tendered by the people the night of my arrival here, or this banquet, are considered by me as intended to be personally complimentary to myself, but recognitions of the principles underlying the Republican party for which this contest was made. A contest for a seat in the United States Senate has seldom caused much popular solicitude, but the protracted controversy, the fact that the parties were equally divided, and the loss of members of the Legislature by death—all conspired to bring the contest prominently to the notice of the people throughout the United States. That the opponents of the Republican party had become at this early day tired of the management of National affairs in the hands of their own friends, is shown in the fact *that they actually staid away from the polls in the Thirty-fourth Senatorial District,* giving us a majority, so that a Republican might again be chosen to represent the State of Illinois in the United States Senate. This has caused the Republicans throughout the country to discover the turn of the tide in favor of Republican principles, and the hearts of all true patriots to leap with joy. To the energy and fidelity of the Republicans of that district are we indebted for this result.

"If I may be permitted to speak of myself in connection with this contest, I will say that I am very much gratified that again I have the honor of representing in the United States Senate this great State with a population of over 3,000,000 intelligent people, with an area of 56,650 square miles, comprising 36,256,000 acres of land, with almost every acre susceptible of cultivation, with more miles of railroad than any other State, and a canal that must become a National highway in the future, whose citizens possess property valued at $3,210,000,000, being the third State in the Union in the production of coal and second in number of universities and colleges, and occupying the same high place in the number of scholars enrolled at school.

"Illinois is varied in its agricultural products, its trade and manufacturing industries, presenting to view a landscape as beautiful as a picture, dotted all over with towns, villages and cities; washed on either side by the two great rivers of our country; with the city of Chicago enthroned on the margin of one of the most beautiful lakes on the continent, possessing a growth, energy, and prosperity which are the marvels of the age. Why should a man not feel a pardonable pride in having been selected as a representative of such a State against combinations of patronage and money, without the influence or use of either? The people of this, my native State, have been more than kind to me in the past. Whether I shall be able to fill the full measure of my public duty, my future must disclose. I can only promise that I shall in all things try to be faithful to their great interests, and do no act that shall cause them to regret the choice they have just made. That I may be able to satisfy my constituents of the honesty of my intentions and to continue in strict devotion to my duties as one of their representatives, is my most ardent desire.

"To the members of the Union League Club, Mr. Chairman, through you, I return my thanks, and with a heart full of gratitude I bow to the people of the State of Illinois."

SENATOR SABIN.

"Senator Sabin of Minnesota was then introduced, and said he was happy to express his deep feelings of gratitude and sympathy which he felt on the occasion which had brought them together. He was glad to offer his congratulations at the termination, so happily and so auspiciously, of one of the most remarkable campaigns that had ever been witnessed upon this continent—a campaign that had been conducted with an honesty of purpose, with an integrity, and with an undying devotion to principle which had signally marked it, and marked the candidate who had been the victor. It had opened to the great Republican party a new life, a new hope; and he congratulated the great State of Illinois and the great Republican party upon this auspicious termination. The fruits of this victory would place the great Republican party, which all honored, and which had not outlived its usefulness, again in the front, and the great State of Illinois—which he was proud to claim as the place of his birth, and which had furnished to the country that grand old hero of Appomattox and the Wilderness, who had so gallantly led the Republican party to victory in the past—would again in 1888 come to the front with her favorite son, and, under his skillful leadership, they should march to victory again."

Congratulatory telegrams to Gen. Logan were read from Judge Harlan, in Milwaukee, and from the Executive Committee of the State Central Committee of California. The Lincoln Club of Meriden, Conn., congratulated the State of Illinois on the election of Gen. Logan. "His victory we deem to be a National blessing," said the letter.

MR. HORR.

"Mr. Horr, of Michigan, said nothing could be more pleasant to him than to be present and congratulate the people of Illinois upon the victory just won. All the Republicans in the State of Michigan were rejoiced at Logan's election, and the few respectable Democrats in that State were equally jubilant. The people of Michigan liked Logan because he struck from the shoulder. He would give more for Logan in the United States Senate than he would for a ten-acre lot of mugwumps. Everybody knew just where to find Logan. Just where to find a mugwump God never knew. At first the contest at Springfield looked very much like a tie, and after the first three months and twenty-nine days it looked to him very much like a tie; and God alone knew where we would have been to-day if the Lord had not mercifully removed Brother Shaw. It was the duty of the Republicans to step in and take advantage of the opening made by the Lord, and they stepped in and took it. Just how they did it he did not know, but it was enough for him to know it was done. His friend at the right (Mr. Medill) had often found fault with the operations of the party. The lesson inculcated by adversity was, that any party which wanted to be successful wanted unification. In regard to the administration of Cleveland, he said it had tried to select in its appointments every man who had tried to break up the government. If they had raked the country with a fine-toothed comb they could not have found any more rabid traitors than had been appointed to office by Cleveland. It had been said that Cleveland had not appointed loyal men to office. He could not have appointed loyal men and stood by the record of the Democratic party. It was disloyal men who elected Cleveland and he was compelled to appoint men of the same stripe. The claim of offensive partisanship was a fraud, and any lukewarm Republican who proposed to remain in office would get left. He hailed the election of Senator Logan as evidence that the Republican party was still on its feet in the United States—as an omen that, three years from now, the Democrats would find the Republicans once more with their armor on; and if the Democrats thought they had a stripling to deal with, before they got through they would find that the Republicans still had sinews in their arms, and, though they had lost one battle, had more strength, more heart, and more determination than ever. Consequently he congratulated the club and the General himself upon the victory, which, to Senator Logan, must be more gratifying than he could express, because he was subjected to such a fight as no man had ever made, in the speaker's memory, in the United States for the office of Senator. Senator Logan went to his duties with the experience of years of service. The speaker had no fears that Senator Logan would ever do anything that would cause the people of Illinois to regret the choice they had made. More than that, the Republicans of the United States felt assured that they had still in the councils of the Nation a man who was always right on all the great questions of the day.

JUDGE SMITH.

Judge Sidney Smith, the next speaker, thought it was refreshing to the people of Chicago, in view of past circumstances, to be able to do honor to a man—a gentleman—who fought battles and won victories by honest work and in daylight. No well-meaning citizen could but feel an interest in the great fight at Springfield. In these unregenerate days it was no ordinary matter to be enabled to do honor to a man who had won on his merits. A man had won without wealth and without patronage in a battle in which fraud and corruption were pitted against him. Though his opponent was an honorable and highminded man, the corrupt rings of the State, with everything at stake, tried to divert the public mind from the real issue. After viewing local politics it was, indeed, a refreshing sight to see a man elected to a public position honestly. "It is difficult for me
—5

to say what position I occupy in local politics," continued the speaker. "I guess I'm a victim of misplaced confidence. Eight weeks ago the polls were closed, yet the result has not been announced." He reviewed the actions of the Council, the delay, the stealing of the ballots, and the fact that the Democrats had been too conscientious to count the votes that they themselves had stolen. He thought that the great victory achieved at Springfield by Gen. Logan would have a salutary effect on city affairs.

JOHN FINERTY.

John F. Finerty was next called upon, and said the banquet was for the purpose of congratulating the unspoiled child of victory. It made no difference whether victor or vanquished, his welcome would have been the same. The victory of Gen. Logan was a good omen, and it would indicate a victory for future years if only the wounds of treason were healed. He claimed, as he had always claimed, that it was not in the power of the party of retrogression to defeat the great Republican party. The conquest just achieved by Gen. Logan has proved it.

REMARKS OF JAMES A. CONNOLLY.

"Twice reaching the dignity of Statehood, Illinois has had much, both of the romantic and of the heroic, in her history.

"In her infancy she grappled with the question of slavery, and after a bitter contest, settled it in favor of freedom.

"When the nation needed defenders on foreign soil, her Hardins and her Bakers, with a chivalry we are proud of, led her young Logan to brilliant victories, which to-day have around them the glamour of romance.

"When, again, the great Republic girded up its loins, and prepared to consummate the work of the revolutionary fathers, all eyes turned to Illinois for a leader in the struggle which was to stop the pen of history for years, awaiting its result, while the world looked on in wonder, as upon an elemental war.

"And here that leader was found, a plain man of the prairies, unlearned in the philosophy of the schools, and unpolished by the hand of social culture.

"His life, his acts, his ending, all making up a heroic romance which carries a lesson to the world.

"Here, too, in the hour of our Nation's supremest peril, the God of our destiny came and picked up a stone, 'rejected by the builders,' which in time became the keystone of that soldierly arch of blue coats that spanned the Nation from the Mississippi to the Atlantic, and made it possible for our Nation to be what it is to-day.

"May the God that lifted him to leadership, and guided him to victory, breathe upon him with healing, and preserve him to the Nation, until in the full ripeness of time he shall be called hence!

"Aye, and the story of the unnamed soldiery of Illinois is one of romance and of heroism, and Illinois can point to the graves of her fallen soldiers on every field of valor in the last great contest and proudly say, 'there be my jewels.' And, too, among all the brave and brilliant volunteer leaders of the late war, the soldiers who carried the muskets and fought the battles, hail our Logan as the chief of them all.

"Whether we see him stretched in his blood, on the field of Donelson, or dashing up the bristling heights of Vicksburg, or rushing like a storm-cloud into battle at Atlanta, he was always a leader in the field, and equally so in the forum.

"This brilliant assemblage of Chicago's leaders does honor to itself in gathering here to-night to honor him for this last great civic victory he has won. But, speaking for Southern Illinois, we begin to fear that you intend to despoil Egypt and adopt him for your own.

"Well, Southern Illinois, while giving him up to Chicago, the matchless queen of the West, will still claim the right to watch after him with the warm affection, the sleepless vigil of the parent for the child—the right to share with you in pride at his success, in admiration for his manly courage and sturdy integrity—and the right to act as color-guard for his banner in every contest.

"This last victory, like all the victories he has won, leaves no stain upon the untarnished shield he has borne so long; it was a victory won in a political contest unmatched in the annals of any State, and about which gathers as much of romance, as about the story of Hooker's battle in the clouds at Lookout Mountain.

"Indeed, toward the close of the long struggle, the Thirty-fourth District became the Lookout Mountain of politics.

"I remember well that November day in 1863, when all the loyal people at the North had their eyes turned toward Chattanooga.

"There, in the valley, was the beaten, beleaguered army of Rosecrans. The Tennessee river behind them, the enemy upon the lofty point of Lookout, and all along the range of Mission Ridge, with their artillery commanding every inch of our camps in the valley.

"Hunger had joined with rebellion to reduce our army in the valley. Chickamauga had been fought and lost, and the hearts of loyal men grew sick, their hopes for the beleaguered army were well-nigh gone, when a quiet, determined leader, fresh from his Vicksburg victory, came to Chattanooga—he reviewed the situation, calmly issued his orders, and disposed his men, until he was ready to move; then starting Hooker up the western slope of Lookout Mountain, bade him fight his way to the top. The daring move was thought to be impossible, and was therefore unexpected by the enemy, but Hooker and his men, inspired by the very audacity of their undertaking, fought their way upward all the hours of that November day, and closed their successful struggle on the mountain top, just as the last rays of the evening sun lit it up, and kissed with victory the flag they unfurled over that eagle's eyrie.

"So in the Senatorial contest just closed. For five weary months the eyes of the whole Nation were turned to Illinois. The Legislature was a tie, but it was hoped by some, and feared by others, that the National administration could in some way use its power to break the tie and elect a Democrat.

"Republicans saw their loss of the United States Senate in the defeat of Logan, and Democrats rejoiced in their anticipated control of that body, by his defeat.

"The President and Cabinet acted as brevet members of the Illinois Legislature in their efforts to defeat Logan.

"The wheels of the National Government were moved or stopped, to suit the emergencies of the Senatorial struggle—the blandishments of power and the temptations of pelf took the place of hunger and rebellion at Chattanooga, to reduce our Republican forces—the preceding November we had fought and lost our political Chickamauga, and hearts grew sore and hopes grew faint among Republicans everywhere ; but Logan, quiet, calm, resolute, was in the valley with his men—his watchful eye saw every weak spot in the lines, his wise counsel and steady courage nerved his loyal forces—he thwarted the plans of the enemy —he kept his men constantly in line, and when the vacancy came in the Thirty-fourth District, he saw his opportunity as the quiet leader from Vicksburg saw his at Lookout Mountain, and while his enemy slept, secure in their majority of 2,000, as Bragg was secure on the cloud-capped top of Lookout, Logan, after distributing his forces, and showing the way to capture the Democratic stronghold, gave the word, and late in the afternoon of that election day, every Republican in that District resolutely pushed forward to the polls, like Hooker's men up the rocky ribs of Lookout, and the last rays of sunlight on that peaceful June evening kissed the Republican banner with a victory as proud, and as fairly won, as Hooker's at Lookout Mountain.

"The capture of Lookout Mountain opened the way for Sherman to Atlanta and to the sea. The capture of the Thirty-fourth District opened the way to Republican success.

"It was the Lookout Mountain of our politics, and all Republicans are proud of the leader who won it.

"The contest had become National in its character, the victory is claimed by the whole Republican party, and to-day the hearts of Republicans are warmed by it from Maine to California.

"We have wiped out the Chickamauga of November last. This battle is the opening of the contest for 1888.

"The long roll has been beaten, our forces are in line, and with a leader such as won the Lookout of the Thirty-fourth District, another November evening's sun will kiss the Republican banner with a victory as grateful to loyal hearts as was Joe Hooker's victory on Lookout Mountain."

LEONARD SWETT.

Leonard Swett said he knew Logan twenty-eight years ago, and he knew him then as a leader of men. He knew Logan afterward as a man of action, and in this sphere Logan was incomparable. In the war Logan was a hero; in the campaign at Springfield he was the conqueror. In the Presidential Convention of 1888 nobody would be surprised to see the name and presence of "Black Jack" Logan at the front. He always "got there."

GEN. SCHOFIELD.

Maj.-Gen. Schofield, the next speaker, said it might, perhaps, be asked what the army had to do with a political love-feast, or what right any representative of it had there, but the answer was: Although the army might not take part in a political contest, the heart of every soldier throbbed with interest and emotion in every great contest in which his fellow-citizens were engaged; and especially when the central figure around which the fight took place was one of his most gallant, beloved fellow-soldiers. He had watched the career of John A. Logan, and stood beside him in some of the fields where he won imperishable renown as a soldier in defense of the cause of his country. He came to-night to join with them as fellow-citizens of Illinois in rejoicing at his triumph. In the remarkable contest just closed, the fidelity to principle, the courage, and the unflinching devotion which had characterized Senator Logan in all his career were not found lacking among those whose duty it was to support him. The speaker joined with those present, without respect to politics, most heartily in rejoicing at the triumph of his fellow-soldier."

JOSEPH MEDILL.

Mr. Joseph Medill spoke substantially as follows:

"*Mr. President:*

"It is too late to call upon me to speak, especially after the eloquent remarks you have heard, and every phase of the subject has been talked out. But you have forced me on my feet and I will say a word or two, if your patience will bear with me. I belong to the party that was founded by George Washington, expounded by Daniel Webster, emancipated by Abraham Lincoln, and saved by Ulysses S. Grant. I have held to the doctrine that every man in the United States, whatever he might call himself, was a Republican who spelled Nation with a large N. My friend Gen. Logan, the hero of many a battle, in early life called himself a Democrat. He was always a Republican at heart, though he knew it not. When the flag of his country was fired upon, the real principles of the man came to the front. Every one who has believed that this country is a Nation in all National affairs, is a Republican. Every one who believes that this Nation is a confederacy of independent States, is a Democrat. That is the real test of party, and has been in this country for 100 years. John C. Calhoun argued out one side of that question; Daniel Webster argued out the other side of it after the Nation was established. Gen. Jackson, who is often called the 'Father of Democracy,' was really a Republican—born, lived, and died one, and if he had had his way freely in his party, if he had had our party behind him, he would have strung on a sour-apple tree, or a higher one, John C. Calhoun, who taught the heresy of State sovereignty. There are tens of thousands of men in the Democratic party to-day who belong to our party. The campaign which has just closed in Springfield, as has been well stated to-night, was the most memorable Senatorial contest in the history of the Republic, and when the news went over the wires last week that John A. Logan had been elected Senator, 5,000,000 men threw up their hats and shouted, and there were thousands of Democrats who were glad in their hearts of the result, which was exactly right. It met the approbation of the American people. Gen. Logan has never failed in any position. It has been well said that we know where to find him. We will know where to find him for the next six years—know where to find him three years and a half from now. It was a bitter draught to be defeated last fall, but the Republican party had held power longer continuously than any party ever held power in a free government since free government was instituted amongst men. I assert that this is its highest encomium—that it is the severest test of the greatness, of the value, of the merit of a party. It has turned over the books to its opponent. It was charged last summer that the Republican party had become corrupted—that the time had come for counting the money—that the people would be startled and amazed, and astonished, and alarmed at the disclosures that would be made. The Democracy had counted the money the Republicans charged themselves with, and found that exactly two cents had rolled under the table. They have gone over the books and discovered nothing to criticise—no rascals, no defaulters, no wrongdoers. No party, after being in power a quarter of a century, has ever turned over the trusts of a great Nation to its successors and shown so clean a record. In my opinion the Republican party will pull itself together, and it will gather back its dissatisfied men, and its doubting Thomases will come home and put their hands in the spearthrust, and find that the party is all right, and that the civil-service reform inaugurated by the Republican party was about as perfect as anything could be. My belief is, that in 1886—less than two years from now—the Republican party will recover control of the popular branch of Congress. They control the Senate by eight majority, and the Supreme Court has not been lost. Two years from now the House of Representatives will join the Senate as a Republican body, I predict. We have now four years to devise true measures and principles for the good of the people, and at the end of four years we will place in the White House one of the candidates of last fall to take up this government for another quarter of a century. The next four years will develop the character of the other party. It will show what they are and what they are not. They have commenced with a blunder, and they are blundering yet. They have put men in power and have carried out their schemes as far as they could; but the people will say: 'Get thee behind me, Satan,' and for four years after 1888 we will have enough chance to undo their errors at the polls last fall; and the people who have been called mugwumps will be the loudest shouters in the camp. They will vote the whole ticket, and they will bring back into the Republican party the men who belong to it and who are outside of it.

And I think, in conclusion, with the utmost certainty of knowledge, based on human nature and the good sense of the American people, that every State which cast its Electoral vote for Fremont, and for Lincoln, and for Grant, and for Garfield, or for Blaine, will cast its Electoral vote for the Republican standard-bearer in 1888; and I believe that by that time the Southern States will be ready to join the Republican column and the principles of the great National Republican party, and that it will continue in power to administer the Government for the good of mankind until the end of the century."

E. G. KEITH.

"Edson G. Keith concluded the speaking with the simple remark that he felt happy that an opportunity was afforded for good men to come together and congratulate themselves on the result of the recent fight in Springfield. As one of the men who differed with Gen. Logan five years ago, in another notable "tiff" at Springfield, he expressed confidence in the hero of the hour. The banquet closed with the singing of 'Auld Lang Syne.'"

Gen. Logan was afterward banqueted in Maine, banqueted in Boston, banqueted in Connecticut, and banqueted wherever he went; and his success was taken as the omen of victory in the future, and the campfires of Republicanism were kindled anew all over this broad land for the campaign of 1888.

CHAPTER VII.

INCIDENTS.

A SICK MEMBER CARRIED SIX MILES ON A LOUNGE.

There are some incidents connected with the contest for United States Senator before the Thirty-fourth General Assembly that are marvels in political management. Representative Brown, of Edwards, was sick at his home, which was six miles distant from the nearest railroad station. Believing that if proper precautions were taken, Mr. Brown might be brought to Springfield in safety, Gen. Logan applied to James McDowell, of Bloomington, to undertake the task. Mr. McDowell left Springfield at 4 P. M., February 10, for the home of Mr. Brown, reaching there the next day, but in order to do so he had to walk nine miles of the way over a rough, frozen road. He found Mr. Brown suffering from pneumonia, but not in a critical condition. After a couple of days' watching and waiting, Mr. Brown informed Mr. McDowell that since a consultation with his wife and family physician he was willing to undertake the journey to Springfield, provided he could be gotten to the railroad station without taking cold, the mercury being below zero. Mr.

McDowell assured him that he had already planned that matter, and accordingly an ordinary lounge was taken and arranged so that eight men could assist in carrying it. A warm, soft bed was made thereon, and on the afternoon of the 12th of February, Mr. Brown was placed upon this bed, warmly blanketed and carefully strapped to the lounge. When ready to start, eight men lifted the burden as easily as though it had been a baby, and gently moved forward for Grayville, while twenty-four others followed as a relief corps. They were three hours and a half in reaching Grayville, but the lounge was not lowered to the ground during the journey. Some officious Democrats of Grayville, finding that Mr. Brown was on his way to Springfield, threatened to indict those who had the matter in charge for manslaughter in case he should die, but Mr. Brown said to them that they need not trouble themselves unnecessarily, as he took all the responsibility himself. On the morning of the 16th of February, at 8 o'clock, Mr. Brown, accompanied by his wife, his family physician, Dr. Hullam, W. W. Brown, a brother, Mr. Jolly and Mr. McDowell, left Grayville in the President's car of the P., D. & E. Railroad, which had been placed at his disposal by Superintendent Geo. L. Bradbury, reaching Springfield at 7 P. M. in even better health than when he had started. He was provided with comfortable quarters at the State House, and attended from day to day the meetings of the Joint Assembly without inconvenience to himself. The presence of Mr. Brown in Springfield enabled the Republicans to vote on joint ballot on the 18th of February, which was the first time either party had been willing to risk a test of strength on joint ballot.

HOW THE SICK MEMBERS WERE BROUGHT IN.

When the hour of noon of February 18th had arrived, it was an interesting sight to witness the bringing in of sick members to attend the meeting of the Joint Assembly. Senator Bridges came tottering in supported by his wife and two friends, while Representative Brown was carried in on a reclining chair. Mr. Bridges' mind had been somewhat paralyzed, and it was with great difficulty, when his name was reached, that he could pronounce the name of Wm. R. Morrison. Mr. Brown, though feeble, responded distinctly at the call of his name, "John A. Logan."

WAS LOGAN ELECTED TWICE?

When the Joint Assembly met on the 18th of February, the roll-call indicated 202 members present. Mr. Sittig, Republican, and Mr. O'Shea, Democrat, were absent. The result of the ballot showed that John A. Logan had received 101 votes, Wm. R. Morrison 94, Elijah M. Haines 4, John Smith 1, scattering 2. Total 202. Mr. Streeter voted for John Smith, and he afterward admitted that he did not have in his mind any particular John Smith. Good parliamentarians claim that Mr. Streeter's vote should have been counted as a blank, and that Gen. Logan was fairly elected by a majority of one, and that the United States Senate would have so held had the case been taken before that body.

SPECIAL ELECTION IN THE THIRTY-FOURTH DISTRICT.

The canvass in the Thirty-fourth District to elect a successor to Mr. Shaw was one of the wonders of the Senatorial campaign. The district is composed of the counties of Mason, Menard, Cass and Schuyler, all of which were Democratic. Arthur A. Leeper was the Democratic candidate and Wm. H. Weaver the Republican. The election took place May 6th, while the Democratic colleague of the deceased Representative was on a pleasure excursion to New Orleans, thus leaving the election, so far as he was concerned, to go by default. The Republicans, on the other hand, improved the opportunity by making what is called a "still hunt," and when the returns came in, to the utter disgust of the Democrats and to the surprise of the Republicans, it was found that Mr. Weaver had carried three out of the four counties—Mason, Menard and Schuyler, thus electing him by a majority of 336. Cass county being the home of Mr. Leeper it was not strange that he should have carried it, but his majority was only 92, being 559 less than Cleveland carried it by. The Democrats of the whole State were deeply mortified at the result, because it gave the Republicans a majority on joint ballot, and thus insured the election of a Republican United States Senator. The leaders determined upon schemes of revolution, and emissaries were sent to each of the counties with the view of prolonging the canvass of the vote to the very latest moment. In the meantime, however, the vote of Schuyler county was promptly canvassed, but as a precautionary measure, the Republican Managing Committee sent to Cass county Senator Mason and Representative Calhoun, and to Mason Representatives Fuller and Messick, and to Menard Representatives Chapman and Snyder, to see that no wrong was committed. The result was that the returns came in all straight, but not until eight days after the election. Had not the Republicans put on a bold front, determined to meet revolution with revolution, Mr. Weaver would never have been permitted to take his seat, under the pretence that he had been elected by fraud.

"HOW WAS IT DONE?"

The great wonder is, how the Republicans carried the Thirty-fourth District, with a Democratic majority of 2,050 to overcome, and where every important town in the entire four counties has its railroads, telegraphs, telephones, press reporters and newspapers. With so many avenues of communication, it is a marvel that the plan of carrying on the campaign did not get to some Democrat somewhere, but so close was the secret kept that but few of the Republican judges of election were aware that the Republicans were running a candidate—indeed, some of them voted for the Democratic candidate. It is, perhaps, true that anybody could have suggested a "still-hunt," but it required wisdom to carry it out successfully, and while the originators of the plan of conducting the contest are entitled to no little credit, yet to the shrewdness displayed by the local managers and the voters themselves is due the great honor of the triumph, for in not a single instance did they uncover to the Democrats their secret, and this victory proved the climax in the election of General Logan.

Some very amusing incidents occurred on the day of the election. At Kilbourn, Mason county, when the canvass of the vote commenced, the first ticket drawn from the ballot-box contained the name of Wm. H. Weaver. The judge, a Democrat, performing this service, said, "We will lay that aside and count it as scattering. Weaver is not running." The second ballot also contained the name of Mr. Weaver, and then the Republican judge suggested, "You had better string those ballots." "String nothing," said the Democrat, "Weaver is not running." But when the count was finished the figures indicated that Mr. Weaver had carried the precinct by a handsome majority.

At another polling place in the same county, the Democratic judges, seeing a few Republicans about, insisted on their voting for Mr. Leeper,
—6

"as they had no candidate of their own." The proffered tickets were accepted, and, being easily exchanged for those containing the name of Wm. H. Weaver, the Republicans then commenced voting as though the Democrats had the only candidate, but when the votes were canvassed, the Democratic judges were greatly chagrined to find that the Republican candidate had carried the precinct. Similar incidents occurred all over the district. And the question remains: "How was it done?"

COUNTED WITHOUT THEIR HOST.

When the Democrats succeeded in prolonging the meeting of the Joint Assembly of May 14th, until after night-time, they had fully made up their minds that they would elect a Senator before morning, through the treachery of Republican members, either by voting directly for the Democratic candidate or for somebody, they did not care whom, so that a quorum was shown as voting. But notwithstanding the Republicans had refrained from voting, all were present that evening except Mr. Sittig, who was in Chicago, and Mr. Hilon A. Parker, who was sick and at his room, but after Mr. Ruger's vote, which made the roll-call within one of a quorum, a messenger was sent for Mr. Parker, who, regardless of his own comfort or health, quickly dressed himself, and made his way to the Joint Assembly, and stood ready to record his vote, had it been necessary. His presence enabled the Republicans to tie the Democrats, but the bold charge of fraud which had been hurled at the Democrats caused them to lose their courage, and the occasion for the Republicans voting did not occur. Evidently, they had counted without their host. We doubt if there ever were so many personal sacrifices made by individual members, that a United States Senator might be elected, as there were during this contest.

A NARROW ESCAPE.

Although General Logan entered the Senatorial contest with the hope of ultimate success, there were times when the stoutest heart would have despaired. The frequent deaths which broke the quorum for weeks and weeks at a time, spread doubt and dismay on all sides. General Logan patiently watched and waited, and waited and watched, never losing hope. But it is related of him that he made up his mind that his election would take place on the 19th of May, or never. The Managing Committee deemed the situation very critical. Representative Barger, who resided in Pope county, where telegraph lines are few and railway trains infrequent, telegraphed Mr. Fuller late Monday evening that he could not be present before Tuesday evening. Mr. McCord, who had been called home by the sickness of his wife's mother, had advised the committee that she was dead, and that he would have to be at her funeral on Tuesday, May 19th. By means of the telegraph and special trains promptly furnished by C. M. Stanton, Superintendent of the O. & M. Railway, Mr. Barger was brought to Springfield at 11 A. M. Tuesday.

The committee wired the situation to Mr. McCord, who, laying the telegram before his grief-stricken father-in-law, James Creel, received this reply: "Go, my son, and do your duty to the State and Nation, and we will bury our dead." With a sad heart, Mr. McCord made his way to Springfield in good season to vote. This made the 103 complete. But it was a narrow escape.

WHY GEN. LOGAN SUCCEEDED.

It has been a marvel to the whole country as to how Gen. Logan succeeded in his Senatorial fight with the odds against him, and unforseen difficulties daily rising before him. Speaker Haines, commenting on the matter, aptly gave the true reason. He said:

"The fight on the part of the Republicans was well managed, in fact their candidate was a General, every member of the managing committee was a General, and the Democrats, without organization, tried to beat them with a lot of corporals, and were defeated."

The Chicago Daily News of May 21st, more than confirms the view of Mr. Haines in the following editorial remarks on the contest which had resulted so disastrously to the Democratic cause:

"The Democratic campaign at Springfield for the past four months has been the old story over again—the old story of lack of leadership and superabundance of insubordination. What leader have the Democrats had at Springfield? Mr. Haines has come nearer than anybody else to being a leader, but his influence was handicapped at the very start by the well-founded belief that he was not a simonpure Democrat. On two or three occasions, Senator Merritt has attempted to take the leadership of the party in hand, but in each instance he evinced simply remarkably erratic powers. There has been no time within the past four months when the Democratic party in the Legislature gave any evidence of being governed by any rules, system, or sense of order. Whenever it voted as a unit it was amid much confusion and frequently under protest, and it seemed as if nothing but the party lash could bring the average Democratic member to terms with his own party and his own interests. At all times the Democrats have brought their grievances into the house and ventilated them there. On the other hand, the Republicans conducted a dignified canvass; whatever family grievances they had were settled among themselves and in their private caucuses. Whenever they came into the State House they stood together and came to the front quietly, decently, and noiselessly. It seemed as if every move they made had been prearranged—nay, more, that it had been rehearsed till every man knew the part he was expected to play. The managers of the Logan canvass at Springfield deserve unqualified praise for the masterly manner in which they organized and controlled the party forces. Never a balk, never a misunderstanding—the smoothness of the four months' campaign was more than admiration, and was wonderful."

ABSTRACT OF SENATORIAL ROLL-CALL.

REMARKS.	Haines voting				Streeter voted for John Smith	Streeter voted for Stevenson, MacMillan for Shuman, and Sittig for Washburne	Same as preceding ballot	Streeter voted for Stevenson, MacMillan for Shuman, and Sittig for Washburne	McMillan voted for Shuman, Sittig for Washburne	Sittig voted for Washburne	Sittig voted for Washburne; MacMillan did not vote
Total votes cast					3,202	3,204	3,204	3,204	3,204	2,204	101
Scattering											
E. Nelson Blake											
Lyman Trumbull											
Wm. Brown											
Wm. M. Springer											
Wm. R. Prickett											
T. E. Merritt											
Wm. J. Allen											
Robert T. Lincoln											
Joseph Robbins											
Richard W. Townshend											
Carter H. Harrison											
John M. Palmer											
Elihu B. Washburne						1	1	1	1	1	1
Andrew Shuman						1	1	1	1	1	
A. E. Stevenson						1	1	1	1		
Richard Bishopp											
Elijah M. Haines					4	4	4	2		2	2
John C. Black											
Lambert Tree											
Wm. R. Morrison	1	1	1	94	94	94	94	95		97	98
John A. Logan				101	100	100	100	100		100	101 100
No. Present on roll-call	200	173	146	182	202	204		204		102	102 102
No. of the ballot	1	2	3	4	5	6	7	8	9	10	11 12
Date of Joint Session	Feb. 13	14	16	17	18	19		20			21

SENATORIAL CONTEST.

Date						1 Haines voting	102 Sittig voted for Washburne	102 Streeter voted for Palmer	102	1 Haines voting	1	1	1	1	100 Powell not voting, Sittig voted for Washburne	2	2	3	1	100	101	101	101	202 Streeter voted for Black, Sittig for Washburne, MacMillan for Blake	201 Streeter voted for Black, Sittig for Washburne, MacMillan for Blake	201 Streeter voted for Black, Sittig for Washburne	202 Streeter voted for Black, Sittig for Washburne	202 Streeter voted for Black, Sittig for Washburne
Feb. 23	131	146				1																							
24	14	125	101																										
25	15	203		98			1	1																					
26	16			98			1	1																					
27	17	200						1																					
28	18	*						1																					
Mch. 2	20	33						1																					
3	21	167						1																					
4	22	191										1	1																
5	23	194																											
6	24	98													1														
7	25	68																											
9	26	73																											
10	27	101										1	1																
11	28	103										1	1	1															
	29											1	1	1	1														
	30											1	1	1	1														
	31											1	1	1	1														
12	32	202		99				1			1																		
	33			98	99																			1					
	34			98	100																				1				
	35			99	100																					1			
	36			99	100																						1		

* No roll-call.

88 SENATORIAL CONTEST.

Abstract of Senatorial Roll-Call—Continued.

Remarks														
		Streeter voted for Black. Sittig for Washburne, MacMillan for Blake	Streeter voted for Black							Streeter voted for Stevenson			Considine voted for Black, Streeter for Stevenson, Mussey for Palmer, Mahoney for Harrison
Total votes cast	202	100	100	100	15	41	1	0	100	100	100	100	100
Scattering	1	1	1	1					1	1	1	1	2
E. Nelson Blake	1												
Lyman Trumbull													
Wm. Brown													
Wm. M. Springer													
Wm. R. Prickett													
T. E. Merritt													
Wm. J. Allen													
Robert T. Lincoln													
Joseph Robbins													
Richard W. Townshend													
Carter H. Harrison												1	
John M. Palmer												1	
Elihu B. Washburne	1												
Andrew Shuman													
A. E. Stevenson								1		1	1	1	
Richard Bishopp													
Elijah M. Haines													
John C. Black	1	1	1			1							1
Lambert Tree						1							
Wm. R. Morrison	99	98	98	98	55	41			98	98	98	94	
John A. Logan	99												
No. present on roll-call		100		49	45	162	188	100	101		101		
No. of the ballot	37	38	39	40	41	42	43	44	45	46	47	48	49
Date of Joint Session	Mch.12	13		14	15	16	17	18	19	20			

		50			92		1			1			1	1					1						4	101	Same as preceding ballot, except that Haines voted for Merritt.
		51			90		1			1			1	1					1						5	100	Same as preceding ballot
		52			89		1			1			1	1					1						5	99	" " "
		53			91		1			1			1	1											5	100	" " "
	21	54	31		19																				1	20	
	23	55	51		21		2																		1	24	Streeter and Darnell voted for Black
	24	56	157		1		1																			2	
	25	57	102	99								1														100	Sittig voted for Washburne
		58		100																						100	
	26	59	104	100								1														101	Sittig voted for Washburne, (MacMillan not voting)
		60		101																						101	MacMillan not voting
		61		100								1														101	Sittig voted for Washburne, (MacMillan not voting)
		62		101																						101	MacMillan not voting
	27	63	81				1																			1	Streeter voted for Black
	28	64	31	1	11																					12	
	30	65	39		4																					4	
	31	66	134				1																			1	
Apr.	1	67	177	1															1							2	Haines voted for Merritt
	2	68	179	2																						2	
	3	69	40	1	15			4																	7	27	
	4	70	23	1	13																				3	17	
	6	71	30	4	19											1									3	27	Collins voted for Robbins
	7	72	48	4	22											1									3	30	" " "
	8	73	106																						1	1	Hereley voted for Wm. E. Mason
	9	74	164				1																			1	
	10	75	127				1																			1	
	11	76	51	2	21		2																		3	28	Streeter and Darnell voted for Black
	13	77	61		22		2									2										26	Streeter and Considine voted for Black, Collins and Rodgers of Warren for Robbins
	14	78	178				1																			1	Streeter voting

SENATORIAL CONTEST.

Abstract of Senatorial Roll-Call—Continued.

Remarks.		Sittig and Ruger not voting		Considine voted for Black		Sheplor voted for L. L. Logan. Sittig and Wheeler not voting.		Rep. Johnson voted for Palmer. Rep. Johnson voted for Palmor. Ruby for Lincoln, and Darnell and Mahoney for Black.	
Total votes cast	1	0	100	100	20	34	0	1	100	100	1	32	17	1	0	0
Scattering					5	2		1				22	6			
E. Nelson Blake																
Lyman Trumbull																
Wm. Brown																
Wm. M. Springer																
Wm. R. Prickett																
T. E. Merritt																
Wm. J. Allen																
Robert T. Lincoln												1				
Joseph Robbins																
Richard W. Townshend						3										
Carter H. Harrison																
John M. Palmer												1	1			
Elihu B. Washburne																
Andrew Shuman																
A. E. Stevenson																
Richard Bishopp																
Elijah M. Haines																
John C. Black						1							2			
Lambert Tree																
Wm. R. Morrison					11	18						9	6			
John A. Logan	1		100	100	4	10			100	100	1		1	1		
No. present on roll-call	196	197	189	100	37	48	144	176	181	100	143	51	38	142	180	180
No. of the ballot	79	80	81	82	83	84	85	86	87	88	89	90	91	92	93	94
Date of Joint Session	Apr. 15	16	17	18	20	21	22	23	24	25	27	28	29	30

SENATORIAL CONTEST. 91

CHAPTER VIII.

CONGRATULATORY TELEGRAMS.

Pittsburg, Pa., May 19, 1885. Gen. John A. Logan: Happy congratulations. Although Blaine and Logan were defeated, Logan to the front. Hip! Hip!
Samuel C. Harris, James D. Long, James H. Murdock.

Princeton, Ill., May 19, 1885. Gen. John A. Logan: Accept our cordial and earnest congratulations on your return to the U. S. Senate. Republicans here are all rejoicing and thanking God and the Thirty-fourth District for your success.
T. J. Henderson, S. G. Paddock, J. W. Bailey, J. W. Templeton, H. M. Trimble.

Chicago, May 19, 1885. Gen. John A. Logan: We join in the hearty congratulations of thousands of Republicans throughout the Union, and hail your victory of to-day as the harbinger of a more glorious one four years hence.
M. A. Mose, Geo. T. Burroughs, J. B. Chambers, James T. Rauleigh, John W. Nundy, H. H. Rice, M. D. Rapp.

Santa Fé, N. M., May 19, 1885. Hon. J. A. Logan: I congratulate you on the glorious result of your magnificent fight.
Wm. W. Griffith.

St. Louis, Mo., May 19, 1885. John A. Logan: The harder the fight the greater the victory. All hail.   P. C. Buckley.

New York, May 19, 1885. Gen. John A. Logan: All join in love and congratulations.   E. Jardine.

Goléonda, Ill., May 19, 1885. Hon. J. A. Logan: We congratulate you upon your success.
J. M. Boicourt, W. H. Boicourt, C. W. McCoy, C. O. Styer, A. G. Pierce.

Buffalo, N. Y., May 19, 1885. Gen. John A. Logan: The Erie County Veteran Logan Legion Club send congratulations.
J. W. Willis, C. A. Orr.

Salt Lake, Utah, May 19, 1885. Gen. John A. Logan: Heartfelt congratulations for your success at last.
John P. Taggart.

Des Moines, Iowa, May 19, 1885. Gen. Logan: Your old comrades in arms and all true blue Republicans in Iowa, send cordial greetings and congratulations.
B. R. Sherman, Governor of Iowa.

Pinckneyville, Ill., May 19, 1885. Hon. J. A. Logan: We congratulate you. God is on our side. Our town is red.
H. P. Huntinger, J. H. Traves, C. H. Roe, M. C. Edwards, Frank Edell, Frank Roe, R. B. Anderson.

SENATORIAL CONTEST. 93

Bloomington. Ill., May 19, 1885. Senator J. A. Logan: I am now content. W. H. H. Adams, Pres't Wesleyan University.

Burlington, Iowa, May 19, 1885. Senator John A. Logan: I am overwhelmed with joy. Please accept my congratulations.
A. M. Adams.

Murphysboro, Ill., May 19, 1885. Gen. John A. Logan: Your old home sends congratulations. G. W. Smith.

East St. Louis,'Ill., May 19, 1885. Senator J. A. Logan: Accept the honest congratulations of Blaine and Logan Club of East St. Louis. Thomas Lefepete, Sec'y.

St. Louis, Mo., May 19, 1885. Hon. J. A. Logan: Congratulations from Mrs. Dooper, Mrs. Paddock and our whole household. Kind wishes to Mrs. Logan. W. R. Paddock.

Grand Rapids, Mich., May 19, 1885. Gen. J. A. Logan: Accept warmest congratulations of Michigan Republicans, including your devoted friend. Wm. A. Gavett.

Streator, Ill., May 19, 1885. Hon. J. A. Logan: Thank God! you are elected at last. All the people say amen.
Ralph Plumb.

Buffalo, N. Y., May 19, 1885. Hon. John A. Logan: Your election is very gratifying to Republicans here. C. A. Orr.

El Paso, Ill., May 19, 1885. John A. Logan: We voted for you, prayed for you, swore by you, and never doubted. We now greet you horizontally and perpendicularly. Fred Cole.

Terre Haute, Ind., May 19, 1885. Gen. J. A. Logan: Cordial congratulations. Glory to God in the highest.
Thomas H. Nelson.

Naperville, Ill., May 19, 1885. Gen. J. A. Logan: Accept hearty congratulations. J. A. Bell.

Harrisburg, Pa., May 19, 1885. Hon. J. A. Logan: We heartily congratulate you on your reëlection to the Senate.
J. W. Lee, E. W. Echols.

Chicago, Ill., May 19, 1885. Gen. John A. Logan: I heartily congratulate you on your well deserved victory.
Alexander Sullivan.

Milwaukee, Wis., May 19, 1885. John A. Logan: The Republicans of the city are jubilant over your election.
E. Sanderson.

Rochester, N. Y., May 19, 1885. John A. Logan: Congratulations on your reëlection to the U. S. Senate. Great rejoicing.
H. Austin Brewster.

Marshalltown, Iowa, May 19, 1885. Gen. John A. Logan: In common with all the Republicans of Iowa, I congratulate you on your splendid victory. Glory! John H. Gear.

Washington, D. C., May 19, 1885. Gen. John A. Logan: Resident Southern Republicans heartily congratulate you on your reëlection. We love you for the enemies you have made.
H. E. Cuney.

Detroit, Mich., May 19, 1885. Gen. J. A. Logan: Words are inadequate to express my great joy. I congratulate you and the country, and thank God. D. V. Bell.

Washington, D. C., May 19, 1885. Hon. John A. Logan: Hearty congratulations on your well earned and well deserved success. John Lynch.

94 SENATORIAL CONTEST.

Sterling, Ill., May 19, 1885. Gen. John A. Logan: Accept my congratulations on your election. Thos. A. Galt.

St. Louis, Mo., May 19. 1885. Hon. J. A. Logan: Accept my own and the congratulations of two hundred thousand other Republicans in Missouri. God bless you. D. P. Dyer.

Chicago, Ill., May 19, 1885. John A. Logan: Hurrah! for the 17th Army Corps, who never surrendered. Have just come from Santa Fé. All well. Geo. C. Ball.

Terre Haute, Ind., May 19, 1885. Hon. John A. Logan: Your friends here rejoice at your election. Accept my sincere congratulations. R. W. Thompson.

Bushnell, Ill., May 19, 1885. Hon. John A. Logan: Your friends here congratulate you upon your election. L. Kaiser.

Chicago, May 19, 1885. Gen. John A. Logan: The private soldiers who fought with you on the bloody field have been with you in this fight in spirit, and we rejoice in your victory.
O. Benson.

West Chester, Penn., May 19, 1885. Gen. John A. Logan: The Veterans' Club of Chester county, Pa., sends congratulations. L. G. McCauley.

St. Louis, Mo., May 19, 1885. Gen. John A. Logan: Hurrah! Missouri soldiers rejoicing over the election of Logan, the Volunteers' General of the war.
Wm. K. Patrick, John S. Cavender, David Murphy, John McNeil.

Albion, Ill., May 19, 1885. Hon. John A. Logan: Let Gabriel blow his horn; I have my robes on. Chas. Churchill.

Marion, Ill., May 18, 1885. John A. Logan: Old Williamson County wants to congratulate you on your glorious victory.
Amzie White.

Alton, Ill., May 19, 1885. John A. Logan: Please accept congratulations of myself and three sons. D. R. Sparks.

Washington, D. C., May 19, 1885. John A. Logan: Congratulations for the general success. Grand Army joins in the glory. John A. Joyce.

Washington, D. C., May 19, 1885. John A. Logan: We congratulate you on your success. Sarville & Staring.

New York, N. Y., May 19, 1885. John A. Logan: I am delighted to learn of your reëlection. J. C. Short.

Carson, Nev., May 20, 1885. Hon. John A. Logan: I congratulate you on your election to the U. S. Senate. Your concluding remarks that you hoped the wrong man had not been elected suits all Republicans here. In the last Presidential contest your name should have been at the head of the ticket, and victory would have been ours. Thos. J. Tennaut.

Washington, Ill., May 19, 1885. John A. Logan: An able defender in a just cause. Your victory is worth millions to the Nation. Accept my heartiest congratulations. Lee Mayer.

Leadville, Col., May 19, 1885. Gen. John A. Logan: Your Republican friends in Democratic Leadville, who gave you eight hundred majority in November, join in congratulations over your great triumph. Representing as you do all that is vital to us, your return to the Senate is peculiarly gratifying.
Geo. W. Cook, C. C. Davis, J. E. Irwin.

SENATORIAL CONTEST. 95

North Gakina, W. T., May 20, 1885. Senator John A. Logan: Heartiest congratulations. Have not been so happy since Appomattox. All honor to Illinois Republicans. Hallelujah!
Thos. H. Cavanaugh.

Rochester, N. Y., May 19, 1885. Hon. John A. Logan: The Young Colored Men's Club of the Powers Hotel has taken a deep interest in your election as U. S. Senator, and therefore takes great pleasure in congratulating you upon your election to-day. G. Thompson, Pres., P. Jones, Treas., R. Thompson, Sec.

Baltimore, Md., May 19, 1885. Hon. John A. Logan: The Logan Invincibles of Maryland organized after the late Presidential election in your honor, to promote the cause of Republicanism. They congratulate you, the State of Illinois, and the United States upon your vindication and election. It is to Maryland Republicans most gratifying.
Thos. R. Rich, R. P. Gorman, Louis Nelke, Frank Warchter.

Cairo, Ill., May 19, 1885. Gen. John A. Logan: Your election makes all Republicans glad in Southern Illinois. Congratulations. C. D. Patier.

Mendota, Ill., May 19, 1885. Gen. John A. Logan: The Republicans of Mendota in mass meeting assembled send greetings and congratulations upon your magnificent triumph. A victory of incorruptible honesty and unswerving integrity to Republican principles over the power of patronage, intimidation and the attempts of corruption and bribery. W. Jenkins.

Morris, Ill., May 19, 1885. Hon. John A. Logan: The flag is flying. Our streets are thronged with people wild with exultation over your election. W. J. Hopkins.

Peoria, Ill., May 19, 1885. Senator John A. Logan: "Faugh-a-Ballugh" for 1888. You are the man for the Irish. James A. Connolly will interpret. P. H. Monahan.

Chicago, Ill., May 19, 1885. Gen. John A. Logan: In honor of your great victory, we have to-day christened a town with the name of Logan, located in San Louis Valley, Colorado, in the center of half million acres of the best land on the continent, and selected and fully endorsed by G. A. R. Department of Colorado for a veteran soldiers' colony, to be known as the Logan Soldiers' Colony. Colorado Colonization Co.

Mansfield, Mass., May 19, 1885. Gen. John A. Logan: The Norfolk Republican Club sends hearty congratulations, and invites you to dinner in honor of the occasion. the date to be named by you. Fred. H. Williams, Sec.

Belleville, Ill., May 19, 1885. Senator Logan: This is a white day in the calendar. So much for pluck and unfaltering trust in principle. We are glad that we have another Republican Senator, and especially glad that you are that Senator.
R. A. Halbert.

Philadelphia, Pa., May 20, 1885. Hon. John A. Logan: We offer our congratulations on your return to the U. S. Senate, knowing as we do, your devotion to the principles of the Republican party, and the decided stand you have taken in behalf of our people. We also congratulate ourselves in knowing there will be one in the Senate of the U. S. that will not turn a deaf ear to the appeals of the one million of colored voters of the Southern States. Gilbert A. Ball, Prest. M. S. I. Club.

Chicago, Ill., May 21, 1885. Gen. John A. Logan: The Republicans of the 15th Ward of Chicago at a large and enthusiastic meeting, held May 20, instructed me to offer you their most hearty congratulations upon your reelection to the U. S. Senate.
John O'Connell, Sect.
William S. Young, Jr., Chairman.

Peoria, Ill., May 19, 1885. Gen. John A. Logan: Accept heartiest congratulations upon your victory, won by indomitable determination, pluck and patience.
Lawrence Harmon.

Paso Payrala, Miss., May 20, 1885. Hon. John A. Logan: I congratulate you and the people of Illinois upon your election.
C. A. Simpson.

Saginaw, Mich., May 20, 1885. Gen. John A. Logan: Your reelection is a national blessing. Accept most sincere congratulations.
David H. Jerome.

Port Huron, Mich., May 19, 1885. Gen. J. A. Logan: Please accept congratulations upon your magnificent triumph.
John P. Sanborn.

Chicago, Ill., May 19, 1885. Gen. John A. Logan: Heartfelt congratulations. Your magnificent leadership has gained the great victory. Chicago Republicans, without division, are proud and happy. A prominent Democratic lawyer said to me to-day, you had fairly won the victory.
R. S. Tuthill.

Galesburg, Ill., May 19, 1885. Hon. John A. Logan: Our whole people join in congratulations. We believe that you will lead the Republicans of the whole Nation to victory in 1888.
Clark E. Carr.

Tuscola, Ill., May 19, 1885. Hon. J. A. Logan: The county that presented the eagle at Decatur sends congratulations, and greets you as her standard bearer for 1888.
Douglas County Republicans.

Chicago, Ill., May 19, 1885. Hon. John A. Logan: Revenge is sweet. Accept all the words of congratulations you can think of in the language.
F. W. Palmer.

Chicago, Ill., May 19, 1885. Gen. J. A. Logan: If your Iowa soldiers' hats were not so high in the air, we would come down and hug the Illinois Legislature.
E. W. Rice.

Chicago, Ill., May 19, 1885. Gen. John A. Logan: Congratulations. The skill with which you have managed your campaign and the righteousness of your course have resulted in a splendid triumph. I am glad.
Burton C. Cook.

St. Paul, Minn., May 20, 1885. Gen. John A. Logan: I congratulate you most heartily upon your reelection to the Senate.
S. I. R. McMillan.

Clinton, Ill., May 19, 1885. Gen. John A. Logan: The Republicans of DeWitt county send greetings. Clinton is celebrating. Flags flying, cannon firing, band playing, and the Republicans are happy.
Richard Butler.

Minonk, Ill., May 19, 1885. Hon. John A. Logan: Accept congratulations. Give us a six years' shake.
M. A. Cushing. E. H. Wilcox.

Chicago, Ill., May 19, 1885. Hon. John A. Logan: On behalf of the entire editorial staff of the Chicago Tribune, I congratulate you on the reelection which you have so well deserved.
R. W. Patterson.

Chicago, Ill., May 19, 1885. Hon. John A. Logan: Distinguished merit triumphs, and forty millions of us shouted Logan. Thomas Dorriss.

Chicago, Ill., May 19, 1885. Gen. John A. Logan: The State owed you the honor she has conferred. She keeps her own honor unstained. Joseph Elyary.

Chicago, Ill., May 19, 1885. Senator John A. Logan. The employés of The Walter A. Wood Mowing and Reaping Machine Company, respectfully tender heartiest congratulations on your richly deserved and brilliant triumph.
Chas. Hamilton.

Chicago, Ill., May 19, 1885. Gen. J. A. Logan: Cleveland confederates and mugwumps mourn. Republicans and patriots rejoice. George P. Jones.

Downers Grove, Ill., May 19, 1885. Gen. John A. Logan: The right must prevail. Warmest congratulations. Hurrah! We extend hands. T. S. and J. W. Rogers.

Chicago, Ill., May 19, 1885. John A. Logan: This beats your past record. To you belongs the credit. Allow me to congratulate you. C. W. Woodman.

Detroit, Mich., May 19, 1885. Gen. J. A. Logan: Hurrah for Logan. Accept congratulations. Wells W. Leggett.

Fairfield, Ill., May 19, 1885. Gen. John A. Logan: Our Republican friends are wild over the results of to-day. It is a grand tribute to your worth as a man and as a party leader. We hold a jollification meeting at the Court House to-night. Shake. Thos. W. Scott.

Lansing, Mich., May 19, 1885. Gen. John A. Logan: Report just received of your victory. Thank the Lord. You have my heartfelt congratulations. R. A. Alger.

Detroit, Mich., May 19, 1885. Gen. John A. Logan: Accept my hearty congratulations. No matter how hard the fight you always win. Henry M. Duffield.

Detroit, Mich., May 19, 1885. Gen. John A. Logan: Congratulations. Michigan rejoices in your election.
I. W. Palmer.

New York, May 19, 1885. Gen. John A. Logan: Pray accept my warmest congratulations on your reëlection to the U. S. Senate. It is a noble testimonial to your patriotism and steadfastness to the glorious principles of the Republican party. Great enthusiasm is manifested, and felicitations are pouring in from all quarters. Simon Stevens.

Oconto, Wis., May 20, 1885. Hon. John A. Logan: We congratulate you most heartily upon your splendid victory and reëlection. It is as it should be, and is an occasion here for great joy among the veterans, some of whom served under you when loyalty was at a premium and disloyalty despised. God bless you. Geo. Beyer, P. H. Swift, W. J. McGue, W. H. Young, O. W. Block, S. W. Fard, A. Cole, O. A. Ellis, W. K. Smith, B. G. Grunert.

Sycamore, Ill., May 19, 1885. Senator Logan: No Rum, Romanism, or Rebellion in this. Shake. R. Ellwood.

Benton, Ill., May 19, 1885. John A. Logan: In the name of Republicans of old Franklin accept congratulations. The God of Israel manifest in Illinois. W. W. Hoskinson.

—7

SENATORIAL CONTEST.

Chicago, Ill., May 19, 1885. John A. Logan: It is a big road for Logan to-day. Accept my warmest congratulations.
Will. N. Eastman.

Philadelphia, Pa., May 20, 1885. John A. Logan: Your comrades in Philadelphia join us in congratulations. To a man up a tree it looks as if the Republicans in Illinois, at least, will be able to compel success.
Louis Wagoner, John Taylor.

Philadelphia, Pa., May 20. 1885. Hon. John A. Logan: Permit us in our own behalf and in behalf of many warm friends of protection to home industry in this city, to congratulate you most heartily upon your reelection to the U. S. Senate.
Samuel M. Patten, Jos. Wharton, Jas. M. Swank.

Philadelphia, Pa., May 19, 1885. Gen. J. A. Logan: Accept the hearty congratulations of the Republicans of our Republican city on the successful termination of your manly fight for right against wrong. The right ever triumphant.
Wm. R. Leed.

Pittsburg, Pa., May 20, 1885. Senator J. A. Logan: Greeting. The Leslie Concert Co. of Chicago are singing, "When John A. Logan's work is done in Washington, there will not be a Democrat to speak the name of Morrison." C. E. Leslie.

St. Ansgor, Ia., May 20, 1885. J. A. Logan: Please accept my hearty congratulations upon your success of yesterday.
Isaac Patterson.

New York, May 21, 1885. Gen. John A. Logan: The Republican members of the New York Assembly in caucus send their hearty congratulations on the occasion of your reelection to the U. S. Senate, and tender their thanks to the Republican Representatives of Illinois for their united and unyielding support of one whose patriotism and fidelity to public trusts have won the regard and confidence of the Republicans in all the States. N. M. Curtis, H. A. Barnum.

St. Louis, Mo., May 19, 1885. Hon. John A. Logan: Congratulations. Besides personal success it is the vindication of regularity and unity indicating well for the future. Mrs. Filley says: Hurrah for the Illinois Republicans.
Chauncy I. Filley.

Moline, Ill., May 19, 1885. Hon. John A. Logan: Your friends here are greatly rejoiced over your election, and extend heartfelt congratulations. Flags are flying and whistles blowing at our factories. Chas. H. Deere, Morris Rosenfield,

New Orleans, La., May 19, 1885. Gen. John A. Logan: Praise God from whom all blessings flow. Congratulate Mrs. Logan for me. Now for 1888. W. P. Kellogg.

Augusta, Maine, May 19, 1885. Gen. John A. Logan: Republicans of Maine send hearty congratulations. Your election is a National victory and means the future success of the party. J H. Manley.

Baltimore, Md., May 19, 1885. John A. Logan: My heartfelt congratulations. Louis Helke.

Boston, Mass., May 20, 1885. John A. Logan: My hearty congratulations on your election. That will make you our next President sure. S. A. Blastand.

SENATORIAL CONTEST. 99

Boston, Mass., May 23, 1885. Hon. John A. Logan: The Massachusetts Club, now at its weekly dinner, sends to you its most cordial congratulations upon your reëlection to the Senate. William Claflin, President,
William W. Doherty, Secretary.

Boston, Mass., May 20, 1885. Hon. John A. Logan: Heartiest congratulations. Our people are thanking God and firing cannons. Geo. F. Hoar.

Boston. Mass., May 20, 1885. Gen. and Mrs. Logan: My hearty congratulations. Frederick Smyth.

Clinton, Ill., May 19, 1885. Gen. J. A. Logan: Accept my congratulations on your election. Hurrah for the Thirty-fourth District. Thos. Snell,

Chicago, Ill., May 19, 1885. Hon. John A. Logan: I congratulate you and the Republican party thoughout the State and Nation. It is the greatest of your many brilliant victories.
J. H. Sanders.

Hinton, West Va., May 20, 1885. Gen. John A. Logan: The Republicans of this section warmly congratulate you upon your success. Theo. Arter, S. F. McBride,
Jas. H. Hobb, Isaac Gorow.

Minneapolis, Minn., May 20, 1885. Hon. John A. Logan. Glory to God. Congratulations from hundreds of your comrades here. Chas. W. Johnson.

London, England, May 20, 1885. Senator Logan: Heartiest congratulations. Morton.

Washington, D. C., May 19, 1885. Gen. John A. Logan: Accept my most cordial congratulations. The contest is unprecedented, and your victory is memorable. James G. Blaine.

Washington, D. C., May 19, 1885. Gen. John A. Logan: You won a national victory. No one rejoices at your election more than W. W. Dudley.

Washington, D. C., May 19. 1885. General John A. Logan: Accept my hearty congratulations upon your reëlection, and Republican victory. Green B. Raum.

Washington, D. C., May 19, 1885. Hon. J. A. Logan: Thank God you were successful. Make my thanks to the friends, one and all, who have stood by you so nobly. Mary S. Logan.

Washington, D. C., May 19, 1885. Hon. John A. Logan: Hearty congratulations. Mrs. Logan is receiving telegrams from all over the country. I. A. Powell.

Philadelphia, Pa., May 19, 1885. Gen. J. A. Logan: Your triumph is glorious. Republican hearts will everywhere beat with joy to-day. Charles Emory Smith.

Eureka Springs, Ark., May 19, 1885. Hon. John A. Logan: Your election takes away the sting of our defeat last November. Hearty congratulations to you and Mrs. Logan.
Powell Clayton.

Nashville, Ill., May 19, 1885. John A. Logan: Washington County Republicans rejoice and congratulate you on being elected U. S. Senator. It is a National triumph. To-night the bands will play and the cannon boom. Hurrah! Hurrah!
L. Krughoff.

100   SENATORIAL CONTEST.

Quincy, Ill., May 19, 1885. Gen. John A. Logan: The Whig most heartily congratulates you on your election. It is a triumph which will result in the greatest good to the whole Nation.
D. Wilcox & Sons.

Homer, Ill., May 19, 1885. Gen. John A. Logan: Accept congratulations from the Republican voters of the Banner Republican township of Champaign county.
J. Thomas, Irvin A. Baker, J. M. Ochiltre.

Santa Fé, N. M., May 19, 1885. Senator John A. Logan: Sincere congratulations. Your friends here, and they are many, rejoice.
Max Frost.

San Francisco, May 19, 1885. Gen. John A. Logan: Heartiest congratulations on your victory. May it be followed by a more glorious one in 1888.
Edward S. Salomon.

Santa Fé, N. M., May 19, 1885. Hon. John A. Logan: Thank God. Right has prevailed. Your friends in New Mexico are rejoicing over your election.
C. B. Hayward.

Albuquerque, N. M., May 19, 1885. Gen. John A. Logan: My heartiest congratulations. The Republican party of the Nation rejoices.
H. M. Atkins.

Albuquerque, N. M., May 19, 1885. Senator John A. Logan: A hundred thousand congratulations.
A. L. Morrison.

Santa Fé, N. M., May 19, 1885. Gen. John A. Logan: My heartiest congratulations on your reëlection as Senator.
A. Staab.

Chicago, Ill., May 19, 1885. Gen. John A. Logan: One of the greatest of your many victories. Chicago jubilant.
P. T. McElherne.

Sullivan, Ill., May 19, 1885. Hon. John A. Logan: The Moultrie County Republicans unanimously congratulate you on your success.
A. Milny.

Anna, Ill., May 19, 1885. Gen. John A. Logan: Republicans of Egypt rejoice over your reëlection. Accept hearty congratulations of a comrade.
L. H. Higgins.

Carlinville, Ill., May 19, 1885. Gen. John A. Logan: "Praise God from whom all blessings flow." Shake.
M. F. Smith.

Youngstown, Ohio, May 19, 1885. Hon. John A. Logan: Congratulations with a big C on your election.
F. S. Presberg.

Geneseo, Ill., May 19, 1885. Senator John A. Logan: To-day's work fitly crowns Illinois' proud Republican political record. Flags flying in behalf of Henry County's five thousand Republican votes. I send you heartiest congratulations.
A. Liberkneck.

Mt. Vernon, Ill., May 19, 1885. Senator John A. Logan: Glory to God in the highest. We all rejoice.
C. W. Pavy.

DuQuoin, Ill., May 19, 1885. Hon. John A. Logan: DuQuoin Republicans congratulate you on your election. Are going to ratify to-night.
S. G. Parks.

Alton, Ill., May 19, 1885. Gen. John A. Logan: Accept our hearty congratulations upon your election.
J. H. and L. D. Yager.

Tuscola, Ill., May 19, 1885. Hon. John A. Logan: I congratulate you heartily. Noble Illinois.
G. M. Abbott.

SENATORIAL CONTEST. 101

Santa Fé, N. M., May 19, 1885. Gen. John A. Logan: My congratulations. All Republicans and all patriots of the country congratulate you most heartily, but themselves and the Nation more. L. A. Shadon.

Santa Fé, N. M.,'May 19, 1885. Gen. John A. Logan: Hurrah for the soldiers' friend. We glory in your success.
G. A. Smith.

Kirksville, Mon., May 19, 1885. Hon. John A. Logan: Nerve and brain win. Congratulations. Praise God for victory.
E. E. Cowperthwaite.

Muskogee, I. T., May 20, 1885. Hon. John A. Logan: Senators Daws and Ingalls send their congratulations. So do I.
James J. Cristie.

Washington, D. C., May 19, 1885. - Hon. John A. Logan: Please accept my hearty congratulations. Alex. Oglesby.

Washington, D. C., May 19, 1885. John A. Logan: A multitude of friends join in congratulating you on your reëlection.
S. D. Rotramel.

Washington, D. C., May 19, 1885. Gen. John A. Logan: I suppose I can congratulate you now. Adams, M. D.

Washington, D. C., May 19, 1885. Hon. John A. Logan: Lizzie joins me in hearty congratulations. In no family except your own is there more rejoicing. Frank Hatton.

Madison, Wis., May 19, 1885. Gen. John A. Logan: Accept my hearty congratulations on your great and deserved triumph. David Atwood.

Washington, D. C., May 19, 1885. Senator John A. Logan: Congratulations on your election. Three cheers for Illinois Republicans. E. W. Whitaker.

Chicago, Ill., May 19, 1885. John A. Logan: I congratulate the Senator-elect, and the next President of the United States.
R. Powers.

McLeansboro, Ill., May 19, 1885. John A. Logan: The Republicans of Hamilton County send greeting to gallant Black Jack Logan. One hundred and three guns are being fired in your honor. C. M. Lyon, C. G. McCoy.

Chicago, Ill., May 19, 1885. John A. Logan: I am profoundly gratified at your success. Another great victory added to brilliant achievements. There will be enthusiastic rejoicing in my household to-night. D. B. Dewey.

Peoria, Ill., May 19, 1885. John A. Logan: I congratulate you most heartily upon your election. A. Stone.

Memphis, Tenn., May 19, 1885. John A. Logan: Your many friends here heartily congratulate you on your victory.
Wm. R. Moore.

Knoxville, Tenn., May 19, 1885. John A. Logan: Accept congratulations. Isham Young, James R. York.

Sheboygan, Wis., May 19, 1885. John A. Logan: The Republicans of Sheboygan congratulate you and the Nation upon your victory. Hurrah for the Black Eagle of Illinois.
Nathan Cole, J. L. Mallory.

Lancaster, Pa., May 20, 1885. Mrs. John A. Logan: Accept my warmest congratulations at the victory long deserved but only yesterday attained by your gallant husband.
H. J. Kauffman.

New York, N. Y., May 19, 1885. John A. Logan: I sincerely congratulate you and the Republican party on your reelection to the U. S. Senate.   George West.

Bingham, Md., May 19, 1885. John A. Logan: Accept my heartfelt congratulations. Better late than never.
John C. Robinson.

Brooklyn, N. Y., May 19, 1885. John A. Logan: Glory to your success.   Jacob North.

New York, N. Y., May 19, 1885. John A. Logan: I have three pictures of you and they are all decorated with flags.
Kilbourn Lennox.

Brownsville, Neb., May 20, 1885. John A. Logan: The Government at Washington still lives. Nebraska sends congratulations. Shake.   D. H. Mercer.

St. Louis, Mo., May 19, 1885. John A. Logan: Congratulations from Pine Ridge Agency.   V. T. Gillyanddy.

St. Louis, Mo., May 19, 1885. John A. Logan: Please accept my warmest congratulations.   Wm. H. Bliss.

Kansas City, Mo., May 19, 1885. John A. Logan: Just heard the good news. Accept sincere and hearty congratulations.   Geo. H. Harlow.

St. Louis, Mo., May 19, 1885. John A. Logan: I congratulate you in the name of all the Republicans of the Exchange.
Nathan Cole.

Kansas City, Mo., May 19, 1885. John A. Logan: Accept congratulations from your friends in Kansas City. You triumphed gloriously.   J. E. Hocsack, Geo. H. Harlow, J. W. Wild, Milton F. Simmons.

Chaura, N. M., May 20, 1885. John A. Logan: Have just received the glorious news from Mary. My hearty congratulations to yourself and the many true friends.
W. F. Tucker.

Santa Fé, N. M., May 19, 1885. John A. Logan: My hearty congratulations.   Mrs. W. F. Tucker.

Chesterfield, Ill., May 19, 1885. John A. Logan: Accept congratulations of the Republicans of Chesterfield on your success.   S. L. Berryman.

New York, May 19, 1885. Hon. John A. Logan: I most heartily congratulate you on your reelection.
Chas. Watrous.

Concord, N. H., May 19, 1885. Gen. John A. Logan: New Hampshire Republicans are joyful over your election. Accept my congratulations on the fitting termination of the long and desperate struggle.   E. H. Rollins.

Maplewood, N. H., May 19, 1885. Hon. John A. Logan: The Republicans of the White Mountains are enthusiastic with delight at your success, and heartily congratulate you.
G. T. Cruft.

Morristown, N. J., May 19, 1885. Gen. John A. Logan: Every loyal heart beats with joy over your reelection. Accept the sincere congratulations of the Republicans of this place.
James C. Youngblood.

Brooklyn, N. Y., May 19, 1885. Senator John A. Logan: With all my heart, I congratulate you on your glorious success.
Henry C. Bowen.

SENATORIAL CONTEST. 103

Brooklyn, N. Y., May 19, 1885. Gen. John A. Logan: God bless you and the men who voted for you. The boys of Brooklyn are the same as ever.
Jas. Ward.

Williamsburg, N. Y., May 20, 1885. Gen. John A. Logan: The Vicksburg of the Democratic party. The Blaine and Logan volunteers extend congratulations upon your success.
John Reitz.

Katouah, N. Y., May 19, 1885. Gen. John A. Logan: I congratulate you with all my heart, upon your reëlection to the United States Senate. It gives great joy to every true Republican.
--W. H. Robertson.

New York, May 20, 1885. Gen. John A. Logan: Congratulations. The Union soldiers shall not always fail in civil life.
H. A. Barnum.

New York, May 19, 1885. Gen. John A. Logan: I congratulate you most heartily on your victory.
L. Hill.

New York, May 19, 1885. Hon. John A. Logan: Justice at last. Republicans elated over your triumph.
R. C. McCormick.

Beatrice, Neb., May 20, 1885. John A. Logan: Five hundred thousand Nebraskans give thanks that our old chief got there.
O. Sabin, W. H. Somers, S. C. Smith.

Omaha, Neb., May 19, 1885. Gen. John A. Logan: We are so glad.
A. Barton, Frankie and Jessie Barton.

Omaha, Neb., May 19, 1885. John A. Logan: The boys are out with forty rounds. The Democratic administration may turn them out, but the people will turn them in.
Pat O. Hows.

Carson, Neb., May 20, 1885. Hon. John A. Logan: Congratulations on your last great victory.
S. L. Lee and C. S. Young.

Canton, O., May 20, 1885. Hon. John A. Logan: Greeting from Third Independent Battery O. V. V. L. A.
W. S. Williams, C. H. Bartlett.

Cincinnati, O., May 19, 1885. Gen. J. A. Logan: I shall be glad to be counted by you as one who rejoices in your election, and the preservation of the honor of your State.
M. Halsted.

Omaha, Neb., May 19, 1885. Gen. John A. Logan: Accept congratulations. Your friends in Nebraska will fire a hundred guns.
Geo. W. E. Darsey.

St. Louis, Mo., May 19, 1885. Senator J. A. Logan: My most hearty congratulations.
E. O. Stanard.

St. Louis, Mo., May 19, 1885. Gen. John A. Logan: Accept my congratulations.
John B. Logan.

New York, May 19, 1885. Hon. J. A. Logan: I heartily congratulate you on your election. You have won a glorious victory.
Charles H. Reed.

New York, May 19, 1885. John A. Logan: A thousand congratulations.
Stephen B. Elkin.

New York, May 19, 1885. Hon. John A. Logan: Permit me to join the public and contribute my most sincere congratulations.
T. C. Platt.

New York, May 19, 1885.• John A. Logan: I congratulate you on a splendid fight and a victory of the greatest National importance and value. John Hay.

Troy, N. Y., May 19, 1885. Gen. John A. Logan: Accept my heartfelt congratulations on your well deserved victory.
Joseph B. Carr.

Oswego, N. Y., May 20, 1885. Gen. John A. Logan: The Empire Republican League, Oswego, New York, congratulate you and the country on your return to the Senate.
A. Cropsey, President.

Buffalo, N. Y., May 19, 1885. Gen. John A. Logan: My mind and heart and all that is within me congratulates you on your grand victory. John M. Farquhar.

New York, May 20, 1885. Hon. John A. Logan: My heartiest congratulations. All Republicans rejoice at your election.
Wm. M. Evarts.

New York, May 20, 1885. J. A. Logan: Congratulations. Now let us have Logan for 1888. James Negley.

New York, May 19, 1885. Hon. John A. Logan: Congratulations of the Irish-American Independents.
Austin E. Ford.

New York, May 19, 1885. Hon. John A. Logan: I congratulate you on your well won victory. Now for 1888.
Patrick Ford.

New York, May 19, 1885. Hon. John A. Logan: Accept my kindest congratulations. Your friends here are jubilant.
Chauncey T. Bowen.

New York, May 19, 1885. Gen. John A. Logan: I sincerely congratulate you. Charles H. Tollis.

Alliance, Ohio, May 20, 1885. Gen. John A. Logan: Congratulations on the result of the long and desperate struggle.
D. M. Sabin.

New York, May 19, 1885. Gen. J. A. Logan: Accept heartiest congratulations on your election to the Senatorship. He laughs best who laughs last. John A. Sleicher, O. G. Warren.

New York, May 19, 1885. Gen. John A. Logan: We offer you our heartfelt congratulations. Wham & Marston.

New York, May 19, 1885. Hon. John A. Logan: We congratulate you most heartily on your election to the Senate. You made a gallant fight, and deserved success.
S. M. Cullom, Warner Miller, C. H. Platt.

Shelbyville, Ill., May 19, 1885. Hon. John A. Logan: We congratulate you on your great triumph. The country looks to you to command the attack in 1888, and meanwhile to check the onward march of the hungry and thirsty Goths and Vandals now rioting on the accumulated gains of twenty-four years of honest and patriotic Republican rule.
Geo. D. Chafee, Sam. H. Webster, Wm. Chew, C. G. Woodward, H. J. Hamlin, J. L. Weakly, Abe Middlesworth.

DeWitt, Mo., May 21, 1885. Hon. John A. Logan: The members of the Estle Post No. 178, G. A. R., send greeting and their congratulations upon your reëlection as U. S. Senator.
Allen D. Richards.

SENATORIAL CONTEST. 105

Zanesville, Ohio, May 19, 1885. Gen. John A. Logan: Accept my congratulations, and through me the congratulations of all Ohio Republicans. Joseph W. O'Neil.

Cincinnati, Ohio, May 19, 1885. Hon. J. A. Logan: Accept hearty congratulations. All Ohio Republicans rejoice because of your election. J. B. Foraker.

Youngstown, Ohio, May 19, 1885. Gen. John A. Logan: The Republicans of Youngstown are wild with joy, because of your election. Accept our hearty congratulations.
L. W. King. O. P. Shaffer.

Fostoria, Ohio, May 19, 1885. Hon. John A. Logan: My hearty congratulations. I am more than gratified.
Chas. Foster.

Springfield, Ohio, May 19, 1885. John A. Logan: I congratulate you on your triumph, and the country will rejoice that you are to be continued in the Senate. J. Warren Keifer.

Cincinnati, Ohio, May 20, 1885. Hon. John A. Logan: Congratulations to you and Mrs. Logan. The interest of the day.
William Henry Davis.

Athens, Ohio, May 20, 1885. Gen John A. Logan: In common with all Republicans, I congratulate you upon your well earned and splendid victory. To the country your election is of far-reaching importance; to you it is a tribute to established merit. Amid our rejoicings, we send greeting to Mrs. Logan, whose place in the affections of the Republican party is not second to her gallant husband. C. H. Grosvenor.

Madison, Wis., May 19, 1885. Gen. John A. Logan: I send you hearty congratulations on your election. J. M. Rusk.

Wilmington, Del., May 19, 1885. Gen. John A. Logan: The Young Men's Republican Club send their heartiest congratulations upon your election as U. S. Senator.
W. R. Benson, Jr.

Cincinnati, Ohio, May 19, 1885. Gen. John A. Logan: Most hearty congratulations. M. F. Force.

Cleveland, Ohio, May 19, 1885. Gen. John A. Logan: Accept my hearty congratulations. Great rejoicing in Cleveland.
"T. N."

Canton, Ohio, May 19. 1885. Gen. John A. Logan: Please accept my heartiest congratulations. Wm. McKinley, Jr.

St. Louis, Mo., May 19, 1885. Hon. John A. Logan: I heartily congratulate you and Mrs. Logan on your election as Senator. It keeps you on the up grade in political life.
S. S. Metcalf.

Kansas City, Mo., May 20, 1885. Hon. J. A. Logan: Congratulations on your well deserved victory.
John W. Murphy, M. M. Ferris.

Edgerton, Mo., May 20, 1885. Hon. John A. Logan: Accept congratulations of D. M. Birch, Post 49 G. A. R., on election.
J. W. Campior,

New York, May 19, 1885. J. A. Logan: Glorious! Your many soldier friends especially rejoice. John W. Vrooman.

Utica, N. Y., May 19, 1885. Gen. John A. Logan: We have fired forty rounds. The old cannon is still full. Our hearty congratulations to you and your noble wife on your glorious victory. Chas. H. Shom, Wm. H. Bright.

SENATORIAL CONTEST.

Albion, N. Y., May 20, 1885. Hon. John A. Logan: Accept of congratulations from a friend and well-wisher.
Daniel O'Leary.

New York, May 19, 1885. John A. Logan: News of your election has just come over the tickers. My heartiest congratulations.
Augustus N. Eddy.

New York, May 19, 1885. Hon. John A. Logan: We are rejoicing over your great victory. Heartiest congratulations.
Whitelaw Reid.

New York, May 19, 1885. Gen. John A. Logan: Accept congratulations. Bully for you, 1888.
S. Ashton.

Youngstown, Ohio, May 19, 1885. Hon. John A. Logan: The Republicans, in county convention assembled, by unanimous vote, instructed me to telegraph you their hearty congratulations upon your reëlection to the Senate, and their best wishes for your future political and general welfare. Louis W. King.

Cincinnati, Ohio, May 20, 1885. Gen. J. A. Logan: I warmly congratulate you on your magnificent victory. Your success will help us greatly in Virginia.
V. D. Grover.

Cambridge, Ohio, May 20, 1885. J. A. Logan: All Republicans congratulate you.
M. D. Robins.

Cincinnati, Ohio, May 19, 1885. Gen. John A. Logan: Congratulations. Justice and right have prevailed at last.
Thos. A. Logan.

Hamilton, Ohio, May 19, 1885. Gen. John A. Logan: Accept my most cordial congratulations.
Chas. E. Giffen.

Warren, Ohio, May 20, 1885. Hon. John A. Logan: With joy we hail your grand victory. Thank the Lord.
John M. Stull.

Cincinnati, Ohio, May 21, 1885. Hon. John A. Logan: The Third Ward Republican Club of Cincinnati extends its hearty congratulations upon your reëlection to the Senate.
J. H. C. Smith. Robert Kirstay.

New York, May 20, 1885. Hon. John A. Logan: I congratulate you. The fight was as bravely made as it was won.
S. D. Phelps.

Clifton Springs, N. Y., May 19, 1885. Hon. John A. Logan: Hearty congratulations on the victory which crowns your brilliant campaign.
Alex. G. Cattell.

New York, May 20, 1885. John A. Logan: Best news since November. Now for 1888.
Wm. Alpin.

Chicago, Ill., May 19, 1885. 'Senator John A. Logan: Accept best and sincere congratulations of your Democratic friend and neighbor.
John A. Makley.

Chicago, Ill., May 19, 1885. Gen. John A. Logan: Heartiest congratulations to you and Mrs. Logan. City wild with joy. Glory!
Simeon W. King.

St. Louis, Mo., May 19, 1885. Senator John A. Logan: Centralians are jubilant, and thank God that Illinois has redeemed herself. Mrs. Sadler joins me in congratulating you.
M. B. Sadler.

Slayton, Minn., May 20, 1885. Hon. John A. Logan: My heart throbs in unison with the whole country. Shake.
W. B. Taylor.

SENATORIAL CONTEST. 107

Fort Snelling, Minn., May 20, 1885. Gen. John A. Logan: Please accept my heartiest congratulations upon your reelection to the U. S. Senate. W. A. Rucke.

Lake Benton, Minn., May 20, 1885. John A. Logan: Accept congratulations of Old Abe Post, No. 39, G. A. R. Old soldiers love you. A. C. Matthews.

Fort Snelling, Minn., May 19, 1885. Gen. John A. Logan: Accept my hearty congratulations, in which Mrs. Moore joins. James M. Moore.

Streator, Ill., May 19, 1885. Hon. John A. Logan: One thousand Streatorites congratulate you on downing the organized obstruction. W. A. Funk.

Canton, Ill., May 19, 1885. Hon. John A. Logan: Accept our heartiest congratulations. The next President of the United States is still the General who never lost a battle when he was in command. C. E. Snively, C. T. Heald, W. H. Shaw, A. B. Smith.

Martinsville, Ill., May 19, 1885. John A. Logan: From a dark corner of Egypt we join in the congratulations of the Republicans of the Nation in your great victory. F. W. Burlingame, Jerry Ishler, H. C. Howell.

Morrison, Ill., May 19, 1885. J. A. Logan: Republicans enthusiastic over your brilliant leadership and success. Flags flying and cannon booming here. Accept my warmest congratulations. Chas. Bert.

Washington, D. C., May 19, 1885. Hon. John A. Logan: I congratulate you, the country and the loyal party of Illinois. You have turned the tide. D. B. Loring.

Washington, D. C., May 19, 1885. Hon. John A. Logan: Words cannot express our joy at your election. Hallelujah! J. H. Baxter.

Washington. D. C., May 19, 1885. Senator John A. Logan: Our warmest congratulations. It was a famous victory. Courage, honorable public service, and statesmanship recognized by Illinois. Robert R. Hitt, Anson G. McCook.

Washington, D. C., May 19, 1885. Gen. John A. Logan: Congratulations. You have won for the National Republican party another Donelson, and you will follow it in 1888 with another Appomattox. George Francis Dawson.

Madison, Wis., May 19, 1885. Gen. J. A. Logan: Republicans here are happy over your election, and one hundred guns are being fired in honor of this National victory. Phil. Spoony.

La Crosse, Wis., May 19, 1885. John A. Logan: Accept congratulations of Mrs. Cameron and myself upon your election. None of your friends rejoice more than we do. Angus Cameron.

Madison, Wis., May 19, 1885. Gen. John A. Logan: Comrade, allow me to congratulate you on your reelection to the Senate. This result is most gratifying to the Republicans of Wisconsin, and particularly so to your soldier comrades. Ernest G. Timme.

Denver, Col., May 19, 1885. Senator John A. Logan: I sincerely congratulate you. W. S. Decker.

Denver, Col., May 19, 1885. Senator John A. Logan; Great honor to you and your steadfast friends. I rejoice.
J. D. Ward.

Denver, Col., May 19, 1885. Senator John A. Logan: Accept my most hearty congratulations in your success in the longest contest on record. H. A. W. Tabor.

Denver, Col., May 19, 1885. John A. Logan: Justice prevailed at last. Glory hallelujah! We congratulate you.
H. Silver.

Denver, Col., May 19, 1885. Hon. John A. Logan: I congratulate you, the Republican party and the Nation, on your election to the Senate. H. W. Teller.

Washington, D. C., May 19, 1885. Hon. John A. Logan: House full of friends rejoicing over your election. Will you not say to each of your friends, including Mr. Barry, that I say, may God bless them? Mary S. Logan.

Chicago, Ill., May 19, 1885. Hon. John A. Logan: Accept the hearty congratulations of Mr. and Mrs. Geo. Gray.

Pontiac, Ill., May 19, 1885. Gen. John A. Logan: Pontiac is wild with joy and excitement at the news of your election. Shake. A. W. Kellogg.

Chicago, Ill., May 19, 1885. Gen. John A. Logan: Congratulations at last. The boys were all there on watch.
Edward Roby.

Mendota, Ill., May 19, 1885. Gen. John A. Logan: I congratulate you. A glorious victory! J. C. Corbus.

Litchfield, Ill., May 19, 1885. Hon. John A. Logan: The Republican club of Litchfield sends enthusiastic greeting.
D. W. Taylor.

Chicago, Ill., May 19, 1885. Hon. John A. Logan: My hearty congratulations. Samuel B. Raymond.

Arcola, Ill, May 19, 1885. Senator John A. Logan: The Republicans of Douglas county send you greeting.
Frank E. Wright.

Peoria, Ill., May 19, 1885. Senator John A. Logan: All Illinois congratulates you on your victory. L. J. West.

Chicago, Ill., May 19, 1885. Gen. John A. Logan: You have never won a more brilliant victory. I congratulate you with all my heart. J. High.

Chicago, Ill., May 19, 1885. Senator John A. Logan: Glory hallelujah! D. Hammon.

Atlanta, Georgia, May 19, 1885. Hon. John A. Logan: We congratulate you on your triumph. God be praised.
J. Norcross, A. E. Buck, John E. Bryant.

Albany, Georgia, May 20, 1885. J. A. Logan: I congratulate you from the bottom of my heart. C. W. Arnold.

Seattle, Washington Ty., May 20, 1885. Hon. John A. Logan: Accept our most hearty congratulations. We all rejoice.
Henry Bash, A. W. Bash.

Hot Springs, Ark., May 20, 1885. Gen. J. A. Logan: Please accept happy congratulations from your grateful friends in Hot Springs. . D. C. Rug, Ellis Wostman, O. R. Lake, J. W. Carhart, D. G. Greaves, C. N. Rix, J. L. Gebhart, H. M. Woodman, J. Reigel, John Howell. J. B. Brooks, J. N. Conger.

SENATORIAL CONTEST. 109

Chicago, Ill., May 19, 1885. Gen. John A. Logan: A thousand congratulations on your glorious victory. I have never been happier in my life. D. E. J. Deering.

Peoria, Ill., May 19, 1885. Senator John A. Logan: Am wearing a new hat. Whoop la! Edward P. Brooks.

New Haven, Conn., May 20, 1885. Senator Logan: Jersey Republicans are proud and happy over your victory, and none more than I. Wm. Walter Phelps.

Hartford, Conn., May 20, 1885. John A. Logan: Mrs. Hawley joins me in most heartily congratulating you and Mrs. Logan upon your brilliant, honorable and important victory.
J. R. Hawley.

Deadwood, Dak., May 21, 1885. Gen. John A. Logan: Accept my most sincere congratulations. Wm. H. Parker.

Washington, D. C., May 19, 1885. Hon. John A. Logan: There is, after all, a God in Israel. Accept my hearty congratulations. Simon Wolf.

San Francisco, May 19, 1885. Gen. John A. Logan: Please accept congratulations of your friend on the Pacific coast.
Wm. Dunn, Jr.

San Francisco, May 20, 1885. Gen. John A. Logan: We send our warmest congratulations, and rejoice with Mrs. Logan with all our hearts. John Pope, P. H. Pope.

Colorado Springs, Col., May 19, 1885. Senator John A. Logan: My warmest congratulations. R. Berney.

Denver, Col., May 20, 1885. John A. Logan: Accept my congratulations. Henry W. Burr.

Denver, Col., May 19, 1885. Mr. and Mrs. Gen. J. A. Logan: Please accept hearty congratulations.
Mr. and Mrs. John L. Routt.

Hot Springs, Ark., May 19, 1885. John A. Logan: Mr. and Mrs. Fleming and Mrs. Greaves join me in congratulations.
D. Greaves.

Georgetown, Col., May 20, 1885. Gen. John A. Logan: Republicans of Clear Creek county heartily congratulate you upon your reëlection to the United States Senate.
A. K. Whit

Redding, Cal., May 20, 1885. Hon. John A. Logan: Republicans of First California Congressional District rejoice at your reëlection. C. C. Bush.

Sanbuena Ventura, Cal., May 20, 1885. Hon. John A. Logan: Please accept most cordial congratulations of
Gen. Wm. Van Dover and Dr. Stephen Bowers.

Hope, Ark., May 20, 1885. Hon. John A. Logan: Accept congratulations on your election for U. S. Senator. Southern Republicans all join therein. Humphrey & Kennedy.

Helena, Ark., May 20, 1885. Gen. John A. Logan: We are proud of the Illinois Republicans who have honored themselves by your election. Jacob Trieber.

Arkansas City, Ark., May 21, 1885. Hon. John A. Logan: As a former citizen of Illinois, and the only Republican member in the Arkansas Senate, permit me to congratulate you.
Henry S. Zane.

Hot Springs, Ark., May 19, 1885. Gen. John A. Logan: We congratulate you most heartily on your election
John Hoffmann, Geo. S. Williams, I. D. Bartlett,

Cairo, Ill., May 19, 1885. Hon. John A. Logan: Egypt congratulates her knight. H. H. Condee.

Chicago, Ill., May 19, 1885. Hon. John A. Logan: Warmest congratulations. John B. Hamilton.

Carthage, Ill., May 19, 1885. Gen. John A. Logan: God knows I congratulate you. A. C. Matthews.

Nashville, Ill., May 19, 1885. John A. Logan: Shake. Everybody happy. T. B. Needles.

Chicago, Ill., May 19, 1885. Hon. John A. Logan: I congratulate you on your election. Pluck will tell.
H. B. Meeker.

Blake City, Ore., May 21, 1885. Hon. John A. Logan: We congratulate you on your great triumph.
J. M. Swift, R. S. Anderson.

Chicago, Ill., May 19, 1885. Senator John A. Logan: Hurrah for "Black Jack." There is a God in Israel, and now for eighty-eight. Gestefield.

Chicago, Ill., May 19, 1885. John A. Logan: You have grandly won a grand victory for the party and yourself. I congratulate you. L. C. Collins, Jr.

Chicago, Ill., May 19, 1885. Gen. John A. Logan: Iowa and all the Northwest are smiling. E. W. Rice.

Chicago, Ill., May 19, 1885. Hon. John A. Logan: Ten thousand congratulations. Emery A. Storrs.

Chicago, Ill., May 19, 1885. Gen. J. A. Logan: A thousand congratulations. When do you leave? Shall I come to Springfield? T. P. Robb.

Crawfordsville, Ind., May 19, 1885. Senator John A. Logan: Accept the hearty congratulations of the entire Republican party in this city, with 103 cheers. J. S. Campbell,
Fred Huestis, Ben Crane,
A. B. Anderson, H. L. Wallace,
C. A. Barker, Harry Pontius,
T. H. B. McCain, John S. Brown.

South Bend, Ind., May 19, 1885. Hon. John A. Logan: Amen to Hon. John A. Logan. Amen to the news from Springfield. Accept our heartiest congratulations.
Clem and P. E. Studebaker.

Topeka, Kas., May 19, 1885. Gen. John A. Logan: There is life in the old land yet. I heartily congratulate you on your magnificent triumph over the allied forces of bourbonism, copper-headism and free-tradeism. John A. Martin.

Harrisburg, Pa., May 19, 1885. Hon. John A. Logan: In common with all Republicans, I rejoice in your reelection. You have my heartiest congratulations. P. L. Magee.

Meadville, Pa., May 19, 1885. Gen. John A. Logan: Congratulations on your splendid victory for the Republican party and yourself. T. L. Flood.

Philadelphia, Pa., May 20, 1885. Hon. John A. Logan: I applaud your persistence and congratulate the country on your victory. Wm. D. Kelley.

SENATORIAL CONTEST. 111

Philadelphia, Pa., May 19, 1885. Gen. John A. Logan: Accept my heartiest congratulations. Capt. Gill.

Bradford, Pa., May 20, 1885. Gen. John A. Logan: It was a glorious victory. Congratulations. W. W. Brown.

Little Rock, Ark., May 19, 1885. Hon. J. A. Logan: Father is visiting us. Brother and wife, self and wife send hearty congratulations. Logan H. Roots.

Salem, Ore., May 21, 1885. Hon. John A. Logan: Accept my hearty congratulations upon your reëlection.
F. F. Moody.

Portland, Ore., May 20, 1885. Hon. John A. Logan: You have won the greatest political battle ever fought. You have our most sincere congratulations. Ben Halladay.

Portland, Ore., May 20, 1885. Hon. John A. Logan: I congratulate you most cordially on the glorious result of your unprecedented contest. J. S. Gage.

Pottsville, Pa., May 19, 1885. Gen. John A. Logan: Accept congratulations. Now for 1888. J. A. M. Passmore.

Danville, Ky., May 20, 1885. John A. Logan: All Southern Republicans greatly encouraged. Hearty congratulations. Logan McKee, Speed S. Fry, J. S. Linney, John W. Frekes.

Topeka, Kan., May 20, 1885. John A. Logan: We congratulate you and your State. E. T. Whitcomb, B. F. Chase.

Owensboro, Ky., May 20, 1885. Gen. John A. Logan: I tender my sincere congratulations to you. Geo. W. Jolly.

Newman, Iowa. May 19, 1885. John A. Logan: Accept congratulations of Iowa Post 323, G. A. R., on your reëlection to the U. S. Senate. Harvey Bare.

Keokuk. Iowa, May 19, 1885. Hon. John A. Logan: The old soldiers of Keokuk send congratulations. Glory to God.
R. Root.

St. Louis, Mo., May 19. 1885. John A. Logan: Victory at last. Accept my congratulations. Your election is a triumph over Democratic frauds, and influence and power of the administration at Washington wielded against you. Therefore, it is doubly gratifying. R. C. Kein.

Chicago, Ill., May 20, 1885. Gen. John A. Logan: By the request of the Bohemian Republicans, I congratulate you on your success, and we hope that we may have a chance to vote for you for the highest office in the Union. Louis Pregler.

Louisville, Ky., May 19, 1885. Gen. John A. Logan: Accept my most cordial congratulations. A fight so fought and so fairly won is worthy of all praise. Walter Evans.

Parsons, Kas., May 20, 1885. Gen. John A. Logan: Accept congratulations of the old soldiers of the Kingdom of Kansas. We are proud and happy. S. W. Kniffin.

Independence, Mo., May 19, 1885. Hon. John A. Logan: Montgomery County Republicans send congratulations.
Yoe.

Lexington, Ky., May 20, 1885. Hon. John A. Logan: My very sincere and cordial congratulations for merited success.
Wm. Cassius Goodlove.

Owensboro, Ky., May 20, 1885. Gen. John A. Logan: The loyal men of Kentucky rejoice over your return to the Senate. Accept congratulations. E. Farley.

Ellsworth, Maine, May 20, 1885. Hon. John A. Logan: My wife and I join in cordial congratulations. Eugene Hale.

Ottawa, Ill., May 20, 1885. Hon. John A. Logan; Mr. and Mrs. S. W. Ruger congratulate you. S. W. Ruger.

Kankakee, Ill., May 19, 1885. Gen. John A. Logan: Accept congratulations of all your friends in Kankakee.
R. J. Hanna.

Dwight, Ill., May 19, 1885. John A. Logan: Republicans of Dwight send you their congratulations. J. B. Parsons.

Quincy, Ill., May 19, 1885. Gen. John A. Logan: Accept our heartiest congratulations on your reelection. Illinois has still forty rounds and is safe. Our best wishes.
E. B. Hamilton, Wm. L. Diston.

Belleville, Ill., May 20, 1885. Gen. John A. Logan: We congratulate you, the party and the country.
M. J. Dobschutz, F. A. McConaughy.

Woodstock, Ill., May 19, 1885. Gen. John A. Logan: Accept congratulations on your glorious victory.
A. S. Wright, Wm. Avary.

Gilman, Ill., May 20, 1885. Hon. J. A. Logan: Hallelujah! Republicans of Gilman all happy. Congratulations.
W. S. Larizon.

Gilman, Ill., May 20, 1885. Hon. John A. Logan: Republicans of Gilman send congratulations to the one hundred and three. Republicans.

Mason City, Ill., May 19, 1885. Hon. John A. Logan: Please accept the earnest congratulations of the Mason City workers of the Thirty-fourth Illinois district. All the Boys.

Chicago, Ill., May 19, 1885. Gen. John A. Logan: Accept my hearty congratulations. Charles Catlin.

Monticello, Ill., May 20, 1885. Hon. John A. Logan: Accept heartiest congratulations for your great victory, from
Monticello High School Republican Boys.

Olney, Ill., May 20, 1885. John A. Logan: We offer you our hearty congratulations on your well-deserved victory, and hope to see you head our ticket in 1888.
H. M. Hall, Chas. Ferriman.

Chicago, Ill., May 19, 1885. Hon. John A. Logan: Please accept my most heartfelt congratulations. Nothing has occurred in years that gives me more pleasure.
Joseph T. Torrance.

Chicago, Ill., May 19, 1885. Hon. John A. Logan: The officers and executive committee of the Young Commercial Republican Club tender their warmest congratulations upon your reelection to the U. S. Senate. H. W. Young.

Chicago, Ill., May 19, 1885. Hon. John A. Logan: Splendid result. Country is to be congratulated. H. U. Higginbotham.

Chicago, Ill., May 19, 1885. Hon. J. A. Logan: Accept my respectful and hearty congratulations on your victory.
Charles M. Dawes.

Chicago, Ill., May 19, 1885. Gen. John A. Logan: Accept sincere congratulations. Father Hodnett.

Chicago, Ill., May 19, 1885. John A. Logan: Allow me to congratulate you on your election. The news gives great satisfaction here. D. W. Irwin.

Rock Island, Ill., May 19, 1885. Gen. John A. Logan: The unanimous vote of a man's party is the highest compliment he can receive. J. G. B.

Albion, Ill., May 19, 1885. Hon. John A. Logan: Accept my warmest congratulations on the happy result to-day.
Chas. Churchill.

Elgin, Ill., May 19, 1885. John A. Logan: Well done. Congratulations. I want to meet you at Chicago.
Nelson Rogers.

Chicago, Ill., May 19, 1885. Hon. John A. Logan: Accept congratulations of your humble servant and your numerous friends at Grand Pacific on your election to the U. S. Senate.
John B. Drake.

Chicago, Ill., May 19, 1885. Gen. John A. Logan: Congratulations. God favors the brave. Sidney Smith.

Chicago, Ill., May 19, 1885. Gen. John A. Logan: Congratulations in the highest degree. O. C. Towne.

Mt. Carroll, Ill., May 20, 1885. John A. Logan: We send greetings. We are happy. - W. D. Hughes.

Rockford, Ill., May 19, 1885. Hon. John A. Logan: Please accept our congratulations. Waite and Wm. A. Talcott.

Chicago, Ill., May 19, 1885. Gen. J. A. Logan: The righteous are never forsaken. My congratulations.
P. W. McWhorton.

Chicago, May 19, 1885. Gen. John A. Logan: The Union League Club of Chicago offers its hearty congratulations to one of its own members upon his reëlection to the U. S. Senate, after a prolonged and arduous contest. The canvass has been a remarkable one, and will become historical on account of its peculiar conditions. It has been conducted in a manner redounding to the credit of each of the contestants. The members of the Club will be happy to have you meet them at a complimentary dinner tendered by the Club on such evening as early as may be convenient to you, and you will confer a favor by designating the time. We have the honor to remain yours very truly, J. McGregor Adams, President.

Joliet, Ill., May 19, 1885. Hon. John A. Logan: Please accept congratulations of the Joliet Barb Wire Co.

Chicago, Ill., May 19, 1885. Hon. John A. Logan: Thanks be to God for victory. Heaven helps those who help themselves. We greet you as the next President of the United States.
E. B. Sherman, G. W. and J. T. Kretzinger.

Wheeling, W. Va., May 22, 1885. Hon. John A. Logan: Heartily congratulating you on your recent victory, and promising to keep a warm spot in our hearts for you in 1888.
Plumed Knights.

Chicago, Ill., May 19, 1885. Hon. John A. Logan: A thousand more congratulations on your deserved victory.
S. W. Kellogg.

Chicago, Ill., May 19, 1885. Gen. John A. Logan: Cordial congratulations. Surely there is a God in Israel. Glory!
Wm. Bross.

Chicago, Ill., May 19, 1885. Hon. John A. Logan: Accept my warmest congratulations on your well-won election as U. S. Senator. M. F. Ludington.

SENATORIAL CONTEST.

Rockville, Ind., May 20, 1885. Hon. John A. Logan: I cordially unite with the host of loyal Republicans in congratulating you upon your deserved success.
John J. Safely.

Warsaw, Ind., May 19, 1885. John A. Logan: Members of the old 15th Army Corps greet you. They feel that they will still have a representative in the U. S. Senate.
Rea C. Williams.

Belleville, Ill., May 19, 1885. Gen. John A. Logan: Allow me to congratulate you on your election.
Chas. Becker.

Prison, Joliet, Ill., May 19, 1885. Senator J. A. Logan: The best we had was forty rounds. They have been fired. Everybody rejoicing. Accept congratulations.
Officers I. S. P.

Chicago, Ill., May 19, 1885. Gen. John A. Logan: I congratulate you and the Republican party on your well-earned and deserved victory.
L. D. Condee.

Chicago, Ill., May 19, 1885. Senator John A. Logan: Accept hearty congratulations.
John T. Long.

Chicago, Ill., May 19, 1885. Hon John A. Logan: Glorious news. Accept the congratulations of yours truly,
A. H. Burley.

Greenville, Ill., May 19, 1885. Senator John A. Logan: The Greenville Blaine and Logan Club sends greetings. You have carried our banner to a magnificent victory. It is national in its results, a grand personal victory to you, and one that we hope will lead to a greater one in 1888.
W. A. Northcott

Richmond, Ind., May 20, 1885. John A. Logan: The Blaine and Logan Glee Club, of Richmond, are singing praises to Illinois.
E. D. Palmer.

Indianapolis, Ind., May 19, 1885. Hon. John A. Logan: Both Mrs. Halford and myself send hearty congratulations. It is a glorious victory, worthily won. Regards to Mrs. Logan.
E. W. Halford.

Indianapolis, Ind., May 19, 1885. John A. Logan: Accept the sincere congratulations of myself and your many friends in Indianapolis.
R. S. Foster.

Terre Haute, Ind., May 20, 1885. Hon. John A. Logan: Accept my congratulations at your triumphant victory.
W. R. McKeen.

Vandalia, Ill., May 19, 1885. John A. Logan: Republicans of Lafayette send congratulations. Glory hallelujah!
R. I. Higgins, D. M. Clark, Fred Remann.

Lafayette, Ind., May 19, 1885. Hon. John A. Logan: Our committee send congratulations. Can you address us on memorial day?
A. L. Stoney.

Indianapolis, Ind., May 19, 1885. Hon. John A. Logan: I congratulate you on your election, the Republicans of Illinois on their pluck and perseverence. Glory!
W. R. Halloway.

Indianapolis, Ind., May 19, 1885. Gen. John A. Logan: I congratulate you and the country on your reëlection. Logan and victory the standard for 1888.
John C. New.

Indianapolis, Ind., May 19, 1885. Hon. John A. Logan: My most cordial congratulations upon your great victory. Indiana Republicans are shouting over it.
B. Harrison.

SENATORIAL CONTEST. 115

Indianapolis, Ind., May 19, 1885. Gen. John A. Logan: I, with thousands of other Republicans, most heartily congratulate you.
J. F. Wildman.

Dubuque, Iowa, May 19, 1885. Gen. John A. Logan: I heartily congratulate you on your election.
W. B. Allison.

Waterloo, Iowa, May 19, 1885. Hon. John A. Logan: Please accept our heartiest congratulations.
Mrs. C. A. Miller, Manning Fish.

Park City, Iowa, May 20, 1885. John A. Logan: Congratulations on your great triumph. Friends greatly rejoice.
W. R. Runtz.

Lafayette, Ind., May 19, 1885. Gen. John A. Logan: Hosts of friends congratulate you on your victory. Now for 1888.
J. M. Dresser.

Green Castle, Ind., May 19, 1885. John A. Logan: Thank God, the country is still safe! We are for you in 1888.
R. M. Black, C. S. Hammond.

Winterset, Iowa, May 23, 1885. Hon. John A. Logan: At a special meeting of the Black Eagle Club, of Winterset, the undersigned was instructed, by resolution, to send the congratulations of the club, and of your friends here, for the brilliant and successful victory achieved over the late Democratic party in Illinois.
W. C. Newlan.

Boone, Iowa, May 20, 1885. John A. Logan: I congratulate you upon again carrying the works.
A. J. Holmes.

Dubuque, Iowa, May 19, 1885. Gen. John A. Logan: Just learned of your election. Dubuque wild with joy and Iowa the same. Sincerest congratulations.
D. B. Henderson.

Humboldt, Iowa, May 20, 1885. J. A. Logan: Three cheers and a tiger. We now count on you for an oration Decoration day.
Albert Rawley.

Petersburg, Ill., May 23, 1885. John A. Logan: The Republicans of the Thirty-Fourth District send greeting. All honor to Illinois' soldier-statesman, John A. Logan.
W. H. Weaver.

LaSalle, Ill., May 19, 1885. Senator J. A. Logan: Hearty congratulations.
J. R. Corbus.

Effingham, Ill., May 19, 1885. Hon. J. A. Logan: Congratulations of Effingham Republicans. One hundred and three guns are now being fired.
Benson Wood.

Chicago, Ill., May 19, 1885. Gen. John A. Logan: Accept best congratulations of family to your well earned success.
Ed. Bert.

Chicago, Ill., May 19, 1885. Hon. John A. Logan: Glory, Glory, hallelujah. Higher yet in 1888.
A. T. Sherman, L. L. Wilson.

Peoria, Ill., May 19, 1885. Gen. John A. Logan: The Republicans of this city congratulate you on your election as one of the sons of Illinois.
S. L. Gill.

Chicago, Ill., May 19, 1885. Gen. John A. Logan: Gallant commander. I congratulate you. God bless you.
P. McGrath.

Chicago, Ill., May 19, 1885. Senator John A. Logan: Accept my congratulations. Every one here seems happy.
Warren F. Leland.

Chicago, Ill., May 19, 1885. Gen. John A. Logan: Only another congratulation and heartfelt felicitation upon your final victory. W. C. Carroll.

Chicago, Ill., May 20, 1885. Senator John A. Logan: Let me congratulate you. I am delighted with your reëlection.
Louis Kistler.

Chicago, Ill., May 19, 1885. John A. Logan: Glory enough. Amen. D. A. Ray.

Winona, Ill., May 19, 1885. Hon. John A. Logan; I hear your are elected. Is it correct? M. Bayne.

Knoxville, Tenn., May 19, 1885. Hon. John A. Logan: The Republicans of Tennessee join the Republicans of the Nation in extending their heartfelt congratulations on your reëlection.
W. P. Brownlow, L. C. Hawk, A. M. Houghes, Jr.

Nashville, Tenn., May 20, 1885. Gen. John A. Logan: The Republican members of the Tennessee Legislature congratulate the country, the Republican party, and yourself on your reëlection to the U. S. Senate, and tender their thanks to the Republicans of the Illinois Legislature for their united support of a faithful and patriotic public servant. S. T. Logan.

Chicago, Ill., May 19, 1885. Gen. John A. Logan: Glory! Congratulations. Country happy. F. M. Bristol.

Chicago, Ill., May 19, 1885. General John A. Logan: I congratulate you with all my heart in your grand victory.
Wm. E. Strong.

Rock Island, May 19, 1885. Gen. John A. Logan: Congratulations and God bless you for 1888. J. M. Beardsley.

Chicago. Ill., May 19, 1885. John A. Logan: With all true patriots and all old soldiers, I rejoice over your success.
D. V. Purington.

Chicago, Ill., May 19, 1885. J. A. Logan: Congratulations.
Geo. Stockton, Ed. Taylor.

Chicago, Ill., May 19, 1885. Gen. John A. Logan: Allow me to congratulate you on your great triumph after such a hard fight. Geo. Schneider.

Harrisburg, Pa., May 21, 1885. Hon. John A. Logan: The Republican Veteran Club of Philadelphia send greetings and congratulations upon your victory over Illinois Democracy.
Terrance T. Osbourn.

Williamsport, Pa., May 20, 1885. Hon. John A. Logan: Just heard of your election. As friends of Blaine and Logan, we congratulate you heartily upon the result. Don't forget the eighty-one thousand Republicans of Pa. and Lycoming county.
C. E. Fritcher.

Chester, Pa., May 20, 1885. Gen. John A. Logan: Accept my warmest congratulations on your reëlection.
Samuel A. Crozer.

Lancaster, Pa., May 19, 1885. John A. Logan: Lancaster county nine thousand majority for Blaine and Logan. Congratulate you on to-day's victory. John A. Hilstand.

Harrisburg, Pa., May 19, 1885. Gen. John A. Logan: Accept my heartfelt congratulations on your having fought the good fight and won. Every man I meet is full of joy at your success.
Henry W. Oliver, Jr.

SENATORIAL CONTEST. 117

Knoxville, Tenn., May 19, 1885. Hon. John A. Logan: The Garfield club send hearty congratulations. R. R. Humes.

Knoxville, Tenn., May 19, 1885. Gen. John A. Logan: Accept congratulations over splendid victory for yourself and Republicans of the Nation. William Rule.

Providence, R. I., May 19, 1885. Gen. John A. Logan: Accept my earnest congratulations on the success you have deserved and won. Nelson W. Aldrich.

Philadelphia, Pa., May 19, 1885. Hon. John A. Logan: The young Republicans of Philadelphia send their congratulations. Edwin S. Stewart.

Creighton, Neb., May 22, 1885. Hon. John A. Logan: Accept congratulations on your reëlection as Senator from one who helped nominate you for the Vice-Presidency, and did his best to elect you. Geo. A. Brooks.

St. Louis, Mo., May 19, 1885. John A. Logan: The campfires will be lighted all over the country. The Republicans, the men who stood by the Nation, rejoice everywhere. Hurrah! Thos. C. Fletcher. Geo. D. Reynolds, A. B. Morrison.

Richmond, Vt., May 20, 1885. Gen. John A. Logan: Vermont Republicans and soldier comrades congratulate you. E. J. Omishee, George Nichols, Redfield Proctor.

Burlington, Vt., May 20, 1885. Gen. J. A. Logan: I congratulate you with all my heart. Geo. F. Edmunds.

Fort Monroe, Va., May 19, 1885. Hon. John A. Logan: My heartfelt congratulations over your success. John F. Dezendorf.

Dallas, Texas, May 19, 1885. Gen. John A. Logan: The Texas Republicans heartily congratulate you and Mrs. Logan. J. C. Bigger.

Terrell, Texas, May 20, 1885. Gen. J. A. Logan: One thousand and one congratulations. O. J. Cropsey.

Philadelphia, Pa., May 19, 1885. John A. Logan: Congratulations. Clover Club anniversary January 14, 1886. You are booked to be there. M. P. Handy, W. R. Balch.

Quincy, Ill., May 19, 1885. Hon. John A. Logan: No other man could have won such a victory. Joseph N. Carter.

Chicago, Ill., May 19, 1885. Hon. John A. Logan: Our hearty congratulations. You are entitled to and have fairly earned the honor. J. B. Hawley, Jas. L. Woodman, Eldridge G. Keith.

Murphysboro, Ill., May 19, 1885. John A. Logan: Congratulations. Mary and Jim.

Murphysboro, Ill., May 19, 1885. John A. Logan: Your election is glory enough for me the balance of my life. F. M. Logan.

Harrisburg, Pa., May 20, 1885. Hon. John A. Logan: The Young Men's Republican Club of Harrisburg extend their hearty congratulations to you, on your recent victory, which is a good omen for 1888. Joseph E. Popel, Chas. Taylor.

Pittsburg, Pa., May 19, 1885. Gen. John A. Logan: My father and myself send congratulations on your brilliant victory. James S. Negley, Jr.

SENATORIAL CONTEST.

Renova, Pa., May 20, 1885. Gen. John A. Logan: Accept congratulations on your reëlection, and pledge of earnest support for President in 1888.
J. N. Bedford, E. C. Young, C. H. Potts.

Chester, Pa., May 20, 1885. Hon. John A. Logan: Bless the Lord for the news. The great Republican party is happy in the success of their leader. We all send greeting. Theo. Hyatt.

New York, May 19, 1885. Hon. John A. Logan: Allow me to congratulate you on winning the biggest political fight I have ever known. Although a Democrat, I am delighted.
S. R. Jerome.

New York, May 19, 1885. Gen. John A. Logan: I congratulate the country and the State of Illinois upon your reëlection.
Byron Andrews.

Albany, N. Y., May 19, 1885. Gen. John A. Logan: The Republicans of New York unanimously and enthusiastically greet you. Brains, courage and integrity invariably win. 1888.
J. W. Husted.

New York, May 19, 1885. Hon. J. A. Logan: Three cheers and a tiger. Congratulations sincere and hearty. The boys have just commenced marching. W. D. Washburn.

Huntington, W. Va., May 20, 1885. Gen. John A. Logan: Joined by the Republicans of Huntington, we most heartily congratulate you. E. E. Ward.

Carbondale, Ill., May 19, 1885. Gen. John A. Logan: Your old home rejoices. Democrats and Republicans send congratulations. E. J. Ingersoll.

Plattsmouth, Neb., May 19, 1885. John A. Logan: The Young Men's Republican Club of Plattsmouth send cordial congratulations to the Black Eagle of Illinois on his brilliant victory. Club.

Omaha, Neb., May 19, 1885. Hon. John A. Logan: My hearty congratulations. Your seat has been kept warm for you with earnest welcome. Charles F. Manderson.

Macomb, Ill., May 19, 1885. Gen. John A. Logan: Glory to God and the Republican party. W. O. Blaisdell.

West Philadelphia, Pa., May 19, 1885. John A. Logan: I am as glad as if it were myself. Thos. Donaldson.

Pittsburg, Pa., May 20, 1885. John A. Logan: I congratulate you on your success. You have merited it.
John Jarrett.

Bradford, Pa., May 20, 1885. John A. Logan: We old soldiers rejoice. "Praise God from whom all blessings flow."
Louis F. Ellis.

Champaign, Ill., May 19, 1885. John A. Logan: This Republican city congratulates you on your reëlection.
B. C. Beach, M. E. Lapham, H. H. Harris, J. B. Harris.

Cincinnati, O., May 19, 1885. John A. Logan: Accept my heartiest congratulations on your reëlection to the Senate.
Henry Simmons.

Cincinnati, O., May 19, 1885. John A. Logan: I extend to you very hearty and sincere congratulations at your deserved success. Abe Mayor.

Chicago, Ill., May 19, 1885. John A. Logan: Glory!
Geo. B. Marsh.

Metropolis. Ill., May 19, 1885. John A. Logan: I congratulate you upon your great victory.
J. C. Willis.

Mason, Ill., May 19, 1885. John A. Logan: Republicans of this part of Egypt congratulate you.
H. C. Henry.

Jerseyville, Ill., May 19, 1885. John A. Logan: Hurrah for Logan and accept congratulations for your brilliant victory.
Morris R. Locke.

Madison, Wis., May 19, 1885. John A. Logan: The Republican Badgers of Wisconsin send greetings to the gallant Republicans of Illinois, and hail your reëlection as Senator as the greatest triumph of the year. Accept my best congratulations.
E. W. Keyes.

New Orleans, La., May 19, 1885. J. A. Logan: We send hearty congratulations, hoping to witness your further election in the future.
A. S. Badger, L. J. Siver, A. H. Leonard.

Santa Fé, N. M., May 19, 1885. John A. Logan: New Mexico rejoices with her favorite chieftain to-day. Illinois forever. Hurrah!
William A. Bailhache, Mason Brayman.

New Orleans, La., May 20, 1885. John A. Logan: Hurrah! Hurrah! Hurrah! So say we all. Kind regards to Mrs. Logan.
F. H. Whitetaker.

Lansing, Mich., May 19, 1885. John A. Logan: The soldiers' hearts beat freer. Michigan veterans congratulate you. Nothing must prevent your being at Portland in June.
C. V. R. Pond.

Burlington, Iowa, May 19, 1885. John A. Logan: Glory hallelujerum. Our flag is still there. Accept congratulations.
A. A. Perkins.

Bangor, Maine, May 19, 1885. Mrs. John A. Logan: At to-morrow's sunrise the birds will be singing from every pine cone in Maine in gladness over the General's latest victory. Mrs. Boutell joins in most heartfelt congratulations.
C. A. Boutell.

Denver, Col., May 19, 1885. Mrs. John A. Logan: Hurrah for Logan.
S. L. Lamon.

San Francisco, May 20, 1885. Mrs. John A. Logan: We rejoice with you with all our hearts. Telegraphed Gen. Logan at Springfield this morning.
C. H. Pope, John Pope.

Monticello, Ind., May 20, 1885. Mrs. J. A. Logan: The old soldiers of White county, Democrats and Republicans, are rejoicing to-night over the success of their old commander.
Committee.

Washington, D. C., May 20, 1885. Mrs. Gen. J. A. Logan: Please accept my hearty congratulations on the grand victory of to-day in Illinois, which assures further Republican victories with Senator Logan as leader. Three cheers for Illinois Republicans.
E. W. Whitaker.

Chicago, Ill., May 19, 1885. Mrs. John A. Logan: We congratulate you upon the splendid triumph of Gen. Logan, and upon the ability which has secured his triumph against great difficulties. Nothing could have given greater delight to the Republicans of Illinois.
B. C. Cook, J. L. High.

SENATORIAL CONTEST.

Chicago, Ill., May 19, 1885. Mrs. John A. Logan: Our love and heartiest congratulations.
Mary A. Bane.

Springfield, Ill., May 20, 1885. Mrs. John A. Logan: Accept the hearty congratulations of your friends on the election of Gen. Logan.
F. P. Snyder.

Springfield, Ill., May 19, 1885. Mrs. John A. Logan: Accept my hearty congratulations at the success of your husband, who never fails when he leads his forces personally.
Wm. F. Harper.

Chicago, Ill., May 19, 1885. Mrs. John A. Logan: Congratulate the General for me. A hard fight, but, thank the Lord, you have won.
L. F. Lindsay.

New York, May 20, 1885. Mrs. John A. Logan: Congratulations. Have so wired the General. The fight was bravely made and won. Republicans here, without exception, join me in good wishes.
S. D. Phelps.

Springfield, Ill., May 19, 1885. Mrs. John A. Logan: Father just elected, and is now addressing Joint Assembly.
John A. Logan, Jr.

Springfield, Ill., May 20, 1885. Mrs. John A. Logan: Now that we are all rested from our grand work, we want to offer you our congratulations on the General's election. Four years hence we are going to visit you at the White House.
Mr. and Mrs. J. B. Messick.

Chaura, N. M., May 20, 1885. Mrs. John A. Logan: Mary telegraphed me the glorious news. My hearty congratulations and love.
W. F. Tucker, Jr.

Assinaboine, Montana, May 20, 1885. Mrs. John A. Logan: Hearty congratulations and best wishes.
J. J. Coppinger.

New York, N. Y., May 19, 1885. Mrs. John A. Logan: Accept my heartfelt congratulations on the General's election.
Wm. H. Marston.

Alexa Bay, N. Y., May 24, 1885. Mrs. John A. Logan: From Ingleside, on the St. Lawrence river, I send you the late but loving congratulations.
Mrs. G. B. Marsh.

New York City, N. Y., May 19, 1885. Mrs. John A. Logan: Senators Cullom, Platt and myself join in hearty congratulations. The General has made a gallant fight and won a great victory.
Warner Miller.

New York City, N. Y., May 20, 1885. Mrs. John A. Logan: We are all made happy in Gen. Logan's victory.
S. J. Shaffer.

Glen Cove, Long Island, May 20, 1885. Mrs. John A. Logan: Congratulations.
Mr. and Mrs. John Birdsall.

New York, May 20, 1885. Mrs. John A. Logan: I congratulate you, the General, the Republican party and the country.
A. McDonald.

Chicago, Ill., May 20, 1885. Mrs. John A. Logan: This illustrious commonwealth has named her distinguished son, your husband, the Hon. John A. Logan, next President of the United States.
Thomas Davis.

Detroit, Mich., May 19, 1885. Mrs. John A. Logan: I am in fullest sympathy with you in rejoicing at your dear husband's election.
Mrs. Thomas W. Palmer.

Springfield, Ill., May 19, 1885. Mrs. John A. Logan: I was elected on first ballot to-day.
John A. Logan.

New York, May 19, 1885. Mrs. John A. Logan: We are delighted to receive the glorious news Warmest congratulations
John W. Vrooman.

Ashtabula, Ohio, May 20, 1885. Mrs. John A. Logan: No one rejoices with you more heartily than your friend,
Betty Kellogg.

Chicago, Ill., May 19, 1885. Mrs. John A. Logan: The weary watch is over and the mists have cleared away. Most heartily do we congratulate you. D. L. and Louis L. Davis.

Springfield, May 19, 1885. Mrs. John A. Logan: General Logan is elected. Chas. H. Crawford.

Ft. Worth, Tex., May 22, 1885. Mrs. John A. Logan: Please accept my sincere and heartfelt congratulations for the General's return to the Senate. M. Jenkins.

New York, May 19, 1885. Mrs. John A. Logan: Allow me to congratulate you and every lover of liberty over the election of your husband. It was a splendid tribute to true patriotism, honesty and heroic manhood. The old comrades of the General are wild with delight. James S. Negley.

www.ingramcontent.com/pod-product-compliance
Lightning Source LLC
Chambersburg PA
CBHW020125170426
43199CB00009B/635